Praise for *Included i*

I can't think of a better combination than a Bible study on Ephesians written by an English professor. Heather's writing style is warm and relatable while delivering the timeless truths of Scripture for which we're so desperate. If you're longing to be chosen, filled, strengthened, and renewed and more, look no further than this study on Ephesians.

KELLY MINTER
Founder and Bible teacher at Cultivate Women's Events
Author of *All Things New*, a study on 2 Corinthians

Heather does a masterful job of bringing the book of Ephesians to life and practice. With authenticity and wisdom, she highlights seven powerful verbs that refocused me on my identity in Christ. As a ministry leader, wife, parent, and friend, I am finding that, by reflecting on those life-giving verbs, I am regaining a renewed sense of His smile and delight.

PATTY RUTTER
Cru, US Leadership Development and HR

We all yearn deeply for value and significance. Heather winsomely guides us through Ephesians to our true identity—being included in Christ.

JENNIFER RICH
Former Cru staff and current therapist/owner at Crossroads Counseling, Ann Arbor, MI

A soul-searching, challenging, but affirming look into the book of Ephesians. Heather's tender heart and transparency leads women to embrace their unique Savior Story in a clear, personal way.

KATRINA CAMPBELL
Christian and Missionary Alliance Women's Ministries, and Alliance Peacemaking

This is the Bible study I've been waiting for! Heather leads us to love grace more, to rest in the power of God's Word, and to more freely and passionately follow our deeply personal Savior in the story He is writing with our lives.

BROOKE BARNETT
Area Director of Cru in Tidewater, VA

Heather Holleman's deep knowledge and application of Scripture, along with her memorable illustrations and use of contrasts, will propel you to a deepening and fulfilling relationship with Christ. You cannot complete this study without your heart and life being captivated and transformed!

MELANIE CRISTE
Director of Women's Ministry, Hunt Valley Church

Included in Christ is a fresh, applicable study for women. We all need to understand the significance of our Savior Stories and the toxicity of our Shadow Narratives. Heather's expertise in the written word helps us to learn and remember His work on our behalf so that we can live in His story with victory.

VICTORIA EVANS PEASLEY
Director of Women's Ministries, Calvary Church of Valparaiso

Get ready for a fresh look at Paul's powerful letter to the Ephesians. Be prepared to walk intimately with God along the way as He helps you see your own story from His perspective. You will love this study.

SUSIE LARSON
National speaker, talk radio host, and author of *Your Powerful Prayers*

Before I was even finished reading the introduction, I wanted to stand up and cheer! God's Word is so full and alive, and seeing these familiar words from Ephesians unpacked this way excites me!

AMY GEIST
Cru at the University of Tennessee, Chattanooga

With refreshing openness, Heather takes us through the book of Ephesians and skillfully guides us to identify the narratives that prevent us from experiencing who we are in Christ and to exchange them with our story of redemption. *Included in Christ* is a life-changing study for all who long to live in the fullness God designed.

PATRICIA HUNTER
Freelance writer, and photographer of *No Matter What, It's a Good Day When*

A well-written study, like a good verb, can change a life. Each time I opened this beautiful book, I envisioned myself seated at a farm table interacting with Heather and Jesus, unpacking vivid verbs and journaling about what God was teaching me. I have been changed.

KOURTNEY GOERGES STREET
Director of Operations, Cru17

My heart, soul, and mind so needed the truths in this study of Ephesians. *Included in Christ* is for every woman who desires to get to the root of her calling and purpose. It's Scripture-saturated, honest, soul-searching, beauty!

LYNDSYE FELSMAN
By Design podcast and blogger

Belonging and acceptance hold sacred space within many of our deepest longings and most painful stories. In Heather Holleman's masterful work, we are invited into a creative and grace-filled journey toward a much sought-after place of rest, safety, grounding, and security. She has woven the gift of our stories, the power of imagery, and the elements of inductive Bible Study into a deep encounter with the metamorphic message in Ephesians that we are always and forever "included."

MEGGAN HUNTOON
Pastor of women and small groups, Cornerstone Church, Boulder, CO

Heather Holleman brilliantly captures the love God has for each of us and the journey we must go on to discover the intimacy in which His love is expressed. This study helps expose the lies we fall prey to, while unfolding the tender truth Jesus wants us to declare about our personal story and relationship with Him.

TRACI HOLLINGSWORTH
Women's coordinator, Woodmen Valley Chapel

INCLUDED *in Christ*

LIVING A NEW STORY FROM EPHESIANS

HEATHER HOLLEMAN

MOODY PUBLISHERS

CHICAGO

All Scripture quotations, unless otherwise indicated, are taken from the Holy Bible, New International Version®, NIV®. Copyright ©1973, 1978, 1984, 2011 by Biblica, Inc.™ Used by permission of Zondervan. All rights reserved worldwide. www.zondervan.com. The "NIV" and "New International Version" are trademarks registered in the United States Patent and Trademark Office by Biblica, Inc.™

Scripture quotations marked NLT are taken from the Holy Bible, New Living Translation, copyright © 1996, 2004, 2007, 2013 by Tyndale House Foundation. Used by permission of Tyndale House Publishers, Inc., Carol Stream, Illinois 60188. All rights reserved.

Scripture quotations marked NASB are taken from the New American Standard Bible® (NASB), Copyright © 1960, 1962, 1963, 1971, 1972, 1973, 1975, 1977, 1995 by The Lockman Foundation. Used by permission. www.Lockman.org.

Portions of Week Three, "Seated," have been used with permission of the publisher from Heather Holleman, *Seated with Christ: Living Freely in a Culture of Comparison* (Chicago: Moody, 2014).

Published in association with the literary agency of D.C. Jacobson & Associates LLC, PO Box 80945, Portland, OR 97280.

Edited by Pam Pugh
Interior and cover design: Erik M. Peterson
Cover image of watercolor tiles copyright © 2017 by petekarici/Getty Images (175523985). All rights reserved.
Author photo: BowerShots Photography

ISBN: 978-0-8024-1591-2

We hope you enjoy this book from Moody Publishers. Our goal is to provide high-quality, thought-provoking books and products that connect truth to your real needs and challenges. For more information on other books and products written and produced from a biblical perspective, go to www.moodypublishers.com or write to:

Moody Publishers
820 N. LaSalle Boulevard
Chicago, IL 60610

1 3 5 7 9 10 8 6 4 2

Printed in the United States of America

To Sarah & Kate

May you always share your Savior Stories

CONTENTS

We teach what we most need to learn.

—Parker Palmer

BEFORE YOU BEGIN

Welcome! I'm thrilled you're here.

I'm so glad you chose to study the book of Ephesians. If I could choose *only one book* of the Bible to study and write about, it would be Ephesians. God used this book in my life to usher in the most profound and lasting personal transformation as I worshiped Jesus, surrendered my life to Him, and understood more clearly the story God has written for our lives. This letter by the apostle Paul—written most likely while he was under house arrest in Rome, around AD 60–62—will tell you who you really are and, most vitally, who Jesus is. It presents the astonishing reality of our being "in Christ" or in some translations, "included in Christ."

We are *included* in Christ, and this changes everything about how we experience God and ourselves in relation to Him.

As we work through this Bible study together, you'll note all the attention to single words and phrases *as if I actually believe they have some kind of special meaning.* The Bible is no ordinary book; we should treat it, not as regular words on a page like the texts I read for my doctorate in literature or as you might read any other source of information, but as the authoritative, inspired words of God. I believe that the words of the Bible, illuminated by the Holy Spirit, serve as our authority and guide for living.

Consider the words Paul wrote in 2 Timothy 3:16–17: "All Scripture is God-breathed and is useful for teaching, rebuking, correcting and training in righteousness, so that the servant of God may be thoroughly equipped for every good work." We need God to help us understand the Scriptures, as when we're told in Luke 24:45 that Jesus "opened their minds so [the disciples] could understand the Scriptures;" and note the prayer from Psalm 119:18: "Open my eyes that I may see wonderful things in your law."

May Jesus open our minds to see Him in Ephesians.

If you are brand new to studying the Bible, or if you just recently acquired your first Bible, you might wonder about what you're holding in your hand. The Bible, simply put, is God's Word that teaches us how to have a relationship with Him through Jesus Christ and enjoy being part of His family forever.

God's Word, by the power of the Holy Spirit, reveals to us our need for a Savior to rescue us from the power and punishment of sin, and it showcases Jesus Christ— God Himself in human form—as the one name under heaven by which we are saved (Acts 4:12). By confessing our sins and receiving the free gift of salvation by faith, we become a child of God.

When we read God's Word, the Holy Spirit teaches, inspires, corrects, and guides us. We read the Bible because it instructs us how to live in the reality of a new kingdom, with a new King, who gives us a brand-new life. We gain a proper understanding of who we are; we learn a new way to connect with others; and we surrender to its truths as a way to truly live well. We also, most important of all, read the Bible to enjoy our relationship with Jesus.

SEVEN IMPORTANT VERBS

Ephesians is a letter from Paul that you can understand best by thinking about seven operative (or most important) words in this short letter. These words happen to be vivid verbs—my favorite! You should know that I study God's Word primarily through analyzing and internalizing verbs. As a college writing instructor, I'm obsessed with *verbs*. I love verbs like grapple, fritter, effervesce. I love verbs that create a mood (how to feel) and an image (what to see). I teach my college writing students to employ precise and vivid verbs in every single sentence.

I collect all the verbs in Scripture that God has used to transform my soul. If you've read my books or heard me speak at Christian conferences, you know I've focused on verbs like *seated, guarded, endure,* and *included* because these are the words God used to change me. And the seven words of our Ephesians study will surely change you as well. What we're going to learn in Ephesians together represents deeply transformational material. I hope that after you complete this Bible study, people will say about you what they said about me: "What has happened to you? You've become a different person!"

You can answer as I did: "I experienced Jesus in a new way through seven verbs of a letter called Ephesians. It changed everything about me."

WHAT YOU'LL NEED

To enjoy this study of Ephesians, you'll need a Bible (I love the NIV, NASB, or ESV translations best, but use your favorite) and something to write on and with (a notebook, journal, pens, or a computer). While the study comprises eight weeks, five days each, feel free to keep your own pace each week and spend more time with days that challenge or inspire you. But on the day your Bible study group gets together, you'll want to have read each day and provided answers to the questions in order to have a great meeting.

To get the most out of this or any Bible study, you need *a willing heart and mind*. In 1 Chronicles 28:9, David offers great wisdom to his son Solomon. I like to think about his words whenever I'm a student in a new setting. David writes,

> And you, my son Solomon, acknowledge the God of your father, and serve him with wholehearted devotion and with a willing mind, for the LORD searches every heart and understands every desire and every thought. If you seek him, he will be found by you; but if you forsake him, he will reject you forever.

Notice those beautiful phrases: *wholehearted devotion and a willing mind*. A willing and teachable heart will open the door for God to perform extraordinary transformation in your life as you study this short letter called Ephesians.

In Jeremiah 29:13–14, the Lord says, "You will seek me and find me when you seek me with all your heart. I will be found by you." Isn't that such a wonderful promise? Imagine the truth of it: If you seek Him in this study, *you will find Him*. He will let Himself be found by you.

WHAT MAKES EPHESIANS SO SPECIAL?

Ephesians isn't a book to take lightly. This is a powerful, direct, and paradigm-shifting book of the Bible. One theologian called the book of Ephesians "the most influential document ever written."[1] Think about that statement in terms of every book ever written in the entire history of the world. For someone to say that this document is the "most influential ever written" is amazing. This same writer said that if we read Ephesians receptively, this book is a "bombshell" in its ability to shape our thoughts and lives.[2]

What I love most about Ephesians—and why it transformed me so powerfully—is that it answers the most fundamental questions about our lives. Who are we? Where do we belong? How shall we live?

Most important, it answers the question of what it means to live "included in Christ" for the rest of our lives.

YOUR STORY

In addition to examining the verbs and key phrases in various sections of Ephesians, I ask questions to help you write the stories that have shaped your life in Christ (as well as the stories that keep you in darkness, not able to fully live out your identity in Him). As you briefly write down the stories that dominate your life and the ones you *wish* to shape your life, you'll grow personally and together with others. Besides delighting in vivid verbs, I'm also an instructor of stories; I teach personal memoir writing and what professionals call the Signature Story for advanced writing students.

The term "Signature Story" means a classic story that best represents who you are—like your handwritten signature. Students write a Signature Story about who they are, why they chose a particular career path, and what event has most shaped their identity and personal mission in life. The Signature Story is usually very short and easily shared in an interview setting. The Signature Story, at least in the business world, also makes a memorable point to inspire and instruct others.

For this study, instead of a Signature Story, we'll create a Savior Story.

The opposite of a Signature Story (or Savior Story) is what we'll call the Shadow Narrative because it's a story that you tell yourself over and over again that keeps you in the darkness of exclusion and loneliness, weariness, and toxic patterns of jealousy, comparison, and despair. I'll share more about both the Savior Story and the Shadow Narrative in Week One. If you're nervous about writing, don't worry. You won't be graded on anything; you don't need to read anything aloud if you don't want to; and you won't have to share your words with anyone if you aren't ready. But you can if you want to, and I hope you will.

You're invited to shares these stories—both the Shadow Narrative and the Savior Story—and listen to other people share theirs. In my ministry role with Cru, so much of my coaching of women involves inviting them to tell a different story about who they are as a new creation in Christ. I began to wonder what it would mean for a woman to live in a different, biblical reality of a new mindset—her Savior Stories—to replace toxic tales of rejection, loneliness, weakness, decay, emptiness, and silence (her Shadow Narratives).

Wasn't the Jesus I met through the book of Ephesians a God who includes us, chooses us, seats us at the table, connects us deeply with others, refreshes us, empowers us, and proclaims truth through us? What if I asked the women I knew to tell those Savior Stories instead of the Shadow Narratives dominating their lives?

THE METHOD OF STUDY

As a college educator with over twenty years of classroom experience, I know that we learn best by comparing and contrasting information and providing images to remember what we're learning. Our brains store knowledge in two forms: linguistic (words) and visual (pictures). And the most fundamental way we learn is by comparing and contrasting information.[3] Paul uses this model all the time as he writes. You'll see it in Ephesians 2 as Paul compares and contrasts the old, dead you to the one alive in Christ. Then he provides memorable images to recall your new identity, whether a seat, a body, a building, or even armor.

Each chapter, therefore, asks us to think carefully about the crucial verb in each section and to picture a scene in our mind about this verb. What ushered in my own fresh experience with Jesus was when I asked the question: *How does a person understanding this verb live?*

So you'll see these questions:

> *How does an included person live?*
> *How does a chosen person live?*
> *How does a seated person live?*
> *How does a strengthened person live?*
> *How does a renewed person live?*
> *How does a filled person live?*
> *How does a proclaiming person live?*

But we answer these questions by first identifying their opposites—the contrast—to enhance how we make sense of our new identity in Christ. You'll see directives like this:

1. Name your Shadow Narrative.

What story do you tell yourself over and over again that keeps you from living this new story? You don't have to spend a lot of time with all the details, but jot down a few lines about the most dominant stories you hold about whatever verb we're discussing.

2. Compose your Savior Story.

What new story has God written—or is He currently writing—about this verb in your life? Set the scene using the five senses to describe yourself and the setting. What was happening (or is happening) in this story that the reader (or listener) needs to know?

3. List the contrasts: How does this new you now live? Compare the old to the new.

   Part of my own work to mature as a Christian was to identify through lists what the "old me" was like. I contrast this with the "new self" of being alive and empowered by Christ.

4. Choose an image or object to remind you of the truth of this verb.

   Images help us recall data quickly and can synthesize massive amounts of data in our brains. I collect many images from the Bible to help me remember the truth of who God is and who I am. I love picturing my "seat" in the heavenly realms, and this past year, I focused on living from the "fortress" of God's care. Now, as you see on the cover of this book, I picture a mosaic to see my included identity.

WHAT MAKES WRITING SO IMPORTANT?

You may wonder why I ask readers to write down the story of their Shadow Narrative. Won't that stir up negative emotions, trauma, and too much pain? What's so important about telling the depressing story that's dominating our lives and preventing us from living our Savior Story?

As both a writing professor and someone who studied the psychology of emotion for five years to earn my PhD (I studied shame and guilt), I've learned the power of writing, sharing our words in community, and revising our stories with a new lens in order to heal from shame and foster intimacy.

Scientific research has confirmed over and over again the benefit of writing down our negative stories. In psychologists James Pennebaker and John Evans's book on expressive writing, they present a fine summary of what so many of us in therapeutic settings have already discovered. They write:

> Since the mid-1980s, an increasing number of studies have focused on expressive writing as a way to bring about healing. . . . Writing for as little as twenty minutes a day for three or four days can produce measurable changes in people's physical and mental health.[4]

We aren't necessarily writing about trauma or horrific events, but the point Pennebaker and Evans make is that writing expressively about negative memories benefits you.

And even if, immediately after writing, the person feels sad (which is normal), within a few hours, those engaged in expressive writing "feel happier and less negative than they felt before writing. Similarly, reports of depressive symptoms, rumination, and general anxiety tend to drop in the weeks and months after writing. Many other studies confirm the improvement in overall well-being, social interactions, and anger management."[5]

My own therapy for six years as I battled depression and anxiety included daily writing. At my blog, *Live with Flair*, I've written daily since March 2010 as a spiritual practice to increase joy, hope, and meaning in my life with Jesus. My own doctors talked about the importance of writing for spiritual health. One showed me the research that said: "Writing in a journal activates the narrator function of our minds. Studies have suggested that simply writing down our account of a challenging experience can lower physiological reactivity and increase our sense of well-being, even if we never show what we've written to anyone else."[6]

THEN WHY DO I STILL NEED JESUS?

At this point, you might wonder, "If positive psychology and cognitive restructuring work so well to make my life happy and meaningful, then why do I need Jesus?" What a great question! As research explodes in the area "narrative identity," people who don't know Jesus and have no interest in Christianity apply the theories of revising personal stories, and they find great success in finding happiness, life purpose, and connection.

Yet such helpful techniques do not, and cannot, solve the problem of sin and separation from God. Positive psychology works as long as your emotions *are all you are*. But as a soul in need of salvation, your positive stories can only take you so far. They cannot repair your relationship with Jesus; right thinking, positivity, and storytelling cannot *forgive sin and lead you to eternity with God in heaven*. Writing can heal some of the symptoms of our sin—our unhappiness, our disconnection from others, and our search for beauty in the midst of pain—but stories won't allow us to do what only the Holy Spirit can do. It is He who makes us alive in Christ and frees us from our enslavement to sin.

We are made for a deeper, more profound, and more incomprehensibly joyful and peaceful experience with Jesus and with one another, and positive psychology represents a mere whisper or shadow of all that awaits you in Jesus. That's why this Bible study excites me so much. It fuses what we know about redemptive personal stories with what Scripture teaches us about the reality of who we really are, and it sets us on the path to live daily in the presence of Him who tells the true story of our lives.

As both a Christ follower and writing professor, I'm thrilled to invite you to write and share as you wish. You don't always have to share your negative stories if it makes you feel uncomfortable, but you are always encouraged to share the Savior Story of God's work in your life through each week of this study. A friend recently said she enjoyed my challenge to transfer her thoughts into words. She writes that "they seem to stick in my mind longer when I do that, and I feel like I am making choices about what I believe and how I want to live when I write or type words."

By the end of this study, you'll quickly identify the ways your Shadow Narratives prevent you from embracing and fully inhabiting the truth of God's Word. And you'll have a new story to tell, your Savior Story, with visual reinforcement, to truly learn from the Scripture.

I'm so excited I can hardly breathe!

As we study Ephesians together and understand our new, shared life in Christ, may our peace, joy, and freedom together abound.

included

An Overview:
Shadow Narratives and Savior Stories

"There is a strain of loneliness infecting many Christians,
which only the presence of God can cure."

—A.W. Tozer

"IN" CHRIST

EPHESIANS 1–2

Read the first two chapters of Ephesians to begin our overview. Underline every time you read the words "in Christ" or "in Him." As you read, think about what it means to be in Christ and how someone becomes included in Him.

This week is your overview—your broad picture—of the book of Ephesians. Before we begin looking carefully at certain passages in each chapter of Ephesians, let me explain why I called this study "Included in Christ." If I were to choose one word to describe Paul's letter to the Ephesians, it would be *included*. Isn't that such a lovely word? To include someone feels so warm and inviting, so much like an enclosing embrace.

As someone who spent a lifetime feeling like an outsider and experiencing rejection—both real and imagined—the notion that I'm *included* reaches my soul like healing balm. For centuries, theologians and scholars have debated the central purpose and big idea of this epistle, and my historical and theological survey textbook tells me that "no unanimity has been reached"[1] about the governing theme of Ephesians.

But when I took a Bible Study Methods course for my seminary training, I couldn't ignore that every chapter hinged for me on that verb "included." This word actually only appears in the New International Version in Ephesians 1:13: "And you also were included in Christ when you heard the message of truth, the gospel of your salvation." In the Greek, the word "included" reads more like "In him you were also." But the sense remains across all translations that "in him you also" means "you were included in all of this."

The notion of being "included in Christ" unifies every chapter of this book. You and I are *included*. We are part of the whole of God's family. Paul's primary purpose in writing Ephesians has everything to do with explaining to readers—and reminding them again and again—that they belong not only in personal and actual union to a living Christ, but that salvation involves including them with one another as believers.

Those of you who love history and context will like this: The beauty and mystery of this book of the Bible is the astonishing invitation that Gentile Christians (once outcasts, non-Jews, not understood as chosen of God) are *included* as fellow citizens with Jewish converts. They are included in the family, part of the household, and resting under God's favor with equal access to every spiritual blessing. Paul wrote this letter to remove any doubt that God's gift of salvation extends to all people, not just the chosen Jews.

Paul wrote this letter to Gentiles—non-Jews—who might have wondered if they really belonged. After all, salvation was for the Jews, right? The Israelites were God's chosen people, right? They were special, favored. And Jews believed that Gentiles were "unclean," so reading that they were now somehow "included" in Christ—that salvation was extended to them, that Jesus could be for them, too, and that they could participate in all the blessings and privileges of being children of God—would have seemed strange, revolutionary even, and then comforting to Gentile readers.

But you have to imagine the context here: Picture the two most opposed groups you can imagine in your community. Think of racial tension, people acting superior to one another, backgrounds and cultures clashing. Consider how a Jew thought it would dishonor God to even eat with—or merely sit at a table with—a Gentile. Imagine sitting with people you consider terribly offensive to you. That's what it was like for Jews and Gentiles to mix.

Ephesians, then, is a grand reconciliation where suddenly it didn't matter what you looked liked, who your parents were, what your social standing was, where you lived, or what your cultural background was. You too were invited into the life of Christ.

If you read this letter through the lens of the Gentile outsider, imagine the words that could come to mind. Excluded. Insecure. Second-best. An afterthought. Maybe they were feeling like they were God's Plan B and invited to the party only because the A-list Jews were disobedient and stubborn.

Have you ever felt like this? Have you ever battled insecurity, rejection, a feeling of worthlessness? Have you been telling yourself the story that you just are not special, favored, chosen, *included*? Have you been living in the Shadow Narrative of your ethnic and family background, limited resources, failures, and limitations that make you feel that you don't belong with all the elite, talented, wealthy, successful, and confident folks?

The real story is that non-Jews were *always included* in God's plan. Gentiles were part of God's salvation story from the beginning and part of His eternal purpose. That's why much of this letter to the Ephesian church uses so many deeply theological words like *predestined* twice in that first chapter. That's also why Paul says that we were chosen "before the creation of the world"—to dissolve any insecurity that someone was only invited as a Plan B. He reminds us that we "also were included in Christ when [we] heard the message of truth."

If you're still confused about this, you can read the prophecy in Isaiah 49:6 about Jesus where God says, "I will also make you a light to the Gentiles, that my salvation may reach to the ends of the earth."

Every time I read the words "you also" in Ephesians, I read it like this: "Yes, you! I really mean you! You're the one! Yes, I'm serious! It's you! You're included! You're chosen, too! It's okay that you aren't this or that. You! I chose you!" So much of this letter cries out for us to know that any one of us feeling excluded or far away from the "in crowd" is now brought into the family.

Paul uses so many beautiful images to help readers cement the truth in their minds: we're seated together (Eph.2:6); we're a household together (2:19); and we're the same body (3:6). Paul essentially instructs readers how to inhabit a new included mindset in those first few chapters.

Instead of rejected, alienated, separated, and lonely, we are now *included.*

What does it mean to be "in Christ"?

How does someone become included in Christ?

What parts of your background and current life experiences make you feel separated from Christ and excluded from the family of God? Write down at least a few sentences, and feel free to journal for at least ten minutes. Think about the setting, characters, and words spoken to you in these Shadow Narratives.

A NEW REALITY

EPHESIANS 3

Read the next chapter of Ephesians (3) to continue our overview, paying special attention to Ephesians 3:2–6.

Underline every time you see the word "together" in Ephesians 3.

Explain in your own words the "mystery of Christ" in Ephesians 3.

This is the new reality: we are *included*. Paul says we are "heirs together with Israel, members together of one body, and sharers together in the promise in Christ Jesus." In case we miss it, he writes *together* three times in this one chapter. We are together with Israel no matter where we came from, who our parents are, or what kind of money we make. We are heirs, just like a natural-born son or daughter.

I love the images that come to mind. I'm thinking of a big dinner table in a spacious Victorian house. I'm also, like Paul, thinking of a building where each brick is a different precious person. I see, too, a beautiful mosaic, like on the cover of this Bible study.

What comes to your mind? Maybe you're thinking of a circle of friends beckoning you to join or a big fluffy couch of family members where there's an empty spot waiting just for you. Everyone is calling your name to include you. You are invited here even if your background, clothing, physical ability, education level, or anything else doesn't match the people around you.

The British historian of missions Andrew Walls wrote something astonishing about Ephesians that ushers this letter into our present reality. He uses the term "Ephesian moment" to signify this present-day miracle of how diverse and irreconcilable communities supernaturally come together through Jesus Christ to manifest His presence.

Walls writes, "None of us can reach Christ's completeness on our own. We need each other's vision to correct, enlarge, and focus . . . ; only together are we complete in Christ."[2] We desperately need each other. You enlarge and focus my vision of Christ.

Perhaps I correct one area of understanding for you, and you show me something new about Jesus at the same time.

Additionally, Walls claims that we are in a new Ephesian moment in light of global Christianity where the largest centers of the Christian faith exist through the African, Chinese, Korean, and Latin American world.[3] What does it mean to participate in the "body of Christ" and live as included with diverse cultures? Walls asks, "Will the body of Christ be realized or fractured in this new Ephesian moment?"[4] Let's think carefully about this question. Will we choose to live included in Christ and with our brothers and sisters in Christ all over the world, no matter who they are or where they originate? Will I look at Jesus through a *global* lens and not just my own small Pennsylvania regional lens?

Ephesians, then, isn't simply about Jews and Gentiles, but it's also about us *right now* living as Christianity expands throughout the whole world. There's a new story to live of interdependence, of an unimaginable togetherness, and of a whole new paradigm of experiencing life.

But before we can live in this new together reality, we have to understand who we are individually in Christ. We need to know the characteristics of our new identity. Paul insists that we live from the new story; we put on the new self instead of living like the old, rejected and lonely us. Our included status now means several new realities. This personal transformation—or a reprogramming of our muddled minds—represents all the new realities of our being "included in Christ." The new realities come straight from each week of our study.

We are now included (Week One), chosen (Week Two), seated (Week Three), strengthened (Week Four), renewed (Week Five), filled (Week Six), and proclaiming (Week Seven). Can you imagine living each day like an *included* person?

Someone *chosen* instead of rejected or ignored?

Someone *seated* at the Greatest Table with the Greatest King instead of lonely and fighting for belonging?

Someone *strengthened* instead of weary and powerless?

Someone *renewed* instead of languishing in sin?

Someone *filled with the Holy Spirit* instead of living in self-effort all day long?

And finally, someone *proclaiming* her Savior Story instead of living in silence or stuck in her Shadow Narrative?

Skim Ephesians again and locate each verb in chapters 4–5. Which parts of Ephesians so far (and which verb) make you most excited to dive into our study?

I pray the changes inside of you come rapidly and permanently as you read the book of Ephesians and let God's powerful, authoritative Word transform your mind. I pray this Bible study goes down in your personal history as a spiritual breakthrough.

WEEK 1 | DAY 3

SPIRITUAL BREAKTHROUGHS

Begin thinking of the story you could share of the first time you felt included in Christ. Write down all the details—the sights, sounds, smells, tastes, and even textures.

What single image comes to mind when you think of the word "included"?

A big group of friends

I experienced a spiritual breakthrough in my burgundy minivan the other day—the same minivan with a dangling front bumper that, were it not for the black electrical tape securing it in place, would fall to the pavement as I drove. While clearly not the most glamorous location for an encounter with God, this minivan served as the setting for a soul-shifting moment.

I had been feeling particularly lonely that morning. I just didn't feel connected in any kind of meaningful way to most people around me. I wondered what other women were doing that day; were they shopping together, eating a delicious lunch, or laughing over Starbucks vanilla lattes and Instagram photos? Sure, I talked with women as I dropped off one daughter at Vacation Bible School and when I saw them at the grocery store in the produce aisle, but I still felt the loneliness of profound disconnection.

It's a terrible feeling. It ranks up there with some of the worst feelings a human can experience.

I'm in the minivan, thinking about my struggle to find deeper connection with folks and those times when my children or I experience loneliness. I'm talking to Jesus as I drive, my eyebrows furrowed and my lips in a frown. I don't want to succumb to this pattern of thinking anymore. I know this feeling like my own skin. This loneliness sends me to tears when I see other communities of people gathering together in friendship. I'll cry at plays and concerts just because I'm imagining the togetherness of the actors and musicians, and there I sit in the audience so lonely there isn't a word for it.

Have you ever experienced this kind of loneliness?

Do I have to live like this? Jesus, what is wrong with me? Is this feeling all in my head? Is my loneliness an actual truth? Is that reality? God, is this true? Or is this a big lie, these feelings and these circumstances? I'm just so lonely and disconnected! What do I do with these feelings?

From somewhere in my brain, I remembered Bible verses about being "included in Christ." I recalled powerful, beautiful, and real pictures from Ephesians of *what is true*: I'm part of a body. I'm seated with Christ. I'm deeply knit in to the family of God. I'm deeply belonging to everyone else, and they belong to me.

I took a deep breath and felt something shift in my soul. The lonely feeling began to fade in light of the truth that I was included and connected to the family of God. I felt like the previously depressed and lonely person in Isaiah 49:21 who was once all alone but who now doesn't know what to do with all the people God has brought into her life. It's a fun little verse to read:

"I was left all alone, but these—where have they come from?"

I remembered my family, my church, neighbors, colleagues, and friends near and far. Suddenly, I was overwhelmed with how deeply related and connected I really was. *Where did all you people come from? I thought I was alone, but I'm not alone at all!*

The great lie is that we're alone, disconnected, alienated, friendless, awkward, and too hopeless for community. It's no wonder. Satan loves to separate people. He's the master of isolation. Satan drives people into solitary places. That's how he works best, like a beast isolating his next victim. Luke 8:29 describes a man who "had been driven by the demon into solitary places." When I realized that part of my old self, flesh, and even Satan desired to drive me to solitary places, I knew I could choose to fight against this plan and fit myself instead into God's design.

I was never actually alone; I simply felt alone. I felt driven to solitary places in my mind. But, by faith, I claimed the truth of who I am. I proclaimed my Savior Story to combat that Shadow Narrative of isolation:

I am not alone now or ever. I'm not disconnected now or ever. I'm not abandoned now or ever. I am in Christ and therefore deeply connected to God and to others. This is the reality of my life.

I exited the vehicle after arriving at Vacation Bible School when it was time to pick up my daughter, and so many wonderful friends and family greeted me with great love. There I stood in my unfashionable khaki shorts and old T-shirt with my brown hair in a messy bun. I told myself:

Now I see it as I've never seen it before. I'm included with these people. We are a family. The spiritual reality of my connection is a truth I know by faith. My feelings and experience may contradict this on bad days, but the truth remains: I am part of a great community in Christ.

Once I choose to believe it, the fiery dart of loneliness and isolation folds and crumbles against my strong and very real shield of faith. This spiritual break-through left me feeling happy because I felt *connected*. I pictured my body having a little rope coming from my middle like a tether connecting me to all the people around me.

I felt happy.

I felt secure.

I felt connected, and nothing had changed about my day. And now that the lonely feeling that kept me isolated left, I knew I had a choice to actively gather with others and live out the truth of my included story. I realized then the truth of the Harvard Grant Study results that I recently read and shared with my Penn State students. As one of the longest-running research projects ever conducted, the Grant Study measured 268 adults for seventy-five years to discover answers to what the key to a happy life is.[5] It wasn't money or success or fame. It wasn't experiences or amenities or any of the things we often seek in life. The single most determining factor, the study found, of happiness and health was one thing: *warm relationships*.

Current lead researcher George Vaillant stated his main conclusion: "Warm intimate relationships are the most important contributing factor in the establishment of a good life."[6] I tell my students at Penn State all about this research, and I pose the question: "What if we measured happiness by how connected we felt to others?" As someone who felt deeply unhappy for many years, I evaluated what contributed most to that state. Indeed, my unhappiness related directly to *disconnection*—from God and from others (and even from myself).

I lost connection.

I wasn't relating to God, and I wasn't in vibrant community. Unhappy people often describe their profound loneliness. They experience isolation and a fractured sense of self. That was how I felt. Maybe you can relate as you read this.

As Christians, we are meant to participate in each other's lives. The Bible talks so much about our togetherness and our interactions with one another. We're *together* a holy dwelling. We're *together* a temple. We're *together* a body and a church. The *togetherness* of Scripture indicates a way we're designed to work best: together.

To see ourselves as entities unto ourselves is a misunderstanding of identity. We're most ourselves when we see our interdependence and communal (rather than isolated) selves. The lonely soul, the isolated soul, quickly experiences desolation. It takes some work and initiative, but we must press on to join community and help others do the same. We thrive and flourish *together*, just as God intended. When one of us suffers or sins, we are all damaged.

Yet American culture offers a full assault on togetherness as we have increasing temptations for isolation (I can do everything online without having to speak to a soul), self-promotion at the expense of community (young adults are taught to develop their personal brand in a world of competition and marketing), pseudo-connection through social media, gossip and comparison, jealousy and division. An important facet of spiritual growth must now include conversations about where and how we're fostering connection instead of isolation and division. We reflect the glory and beauty of God in our togetherness, so we must fight against those things that divide and isolate us.

List some of the ways you actively foster isolation in your life. Now list some of the ways you currently foster—or intend to foster—connection with the body of Christ.

Reread Ephesians 4–5. Make a list of how Paul's commands help foster connection with people. According to your list, make a column of opposite behaviors that threaten "togetherness."

Bear with one another in love	bitterness
bond of peace	rage
speak truth in love	malice
speak truthfully	
kind & compassionate	
respect your husband	

THE PROBLEM OF LONELINESS AND DISCONNECTION

Finish our overview of Ephesians by reading chapter 6. Continue to think about loneliness and disconnection as Satan's strategy to attack God's people.

Recently the *New York Times* named our problem an "epidemic of loneliness"[7] and *Time* claimed that loneliness might be the next biggest public health issue.[8] It's no wonder, therefore, that many researchers currently explore chronic disconnection because of our culture of isolation, independence, competition. A national survey of college students in Canada reported the news that 70 percent of college students battled loneliness, claiming to feel "very lonely" and "so depressed that it was difficult to function."[9]

Amy Banks, a psychiatrist who wrote *Wired to Connect*, claims: "One of the things that happens when you get into a hyper-individualized society is you begin to take relationship out of the equation of what stimulates dopamine. And then, people want the dopamine and replace it with another thing to do repeatedly."[10] To stimulate the dopamine we miss through relational interactions, we might overwork, overeat, or engage in sinful behavior over and over again.

Banks's research proves that relationships, not isolation, stand at the core of human health and well-being. She even makes this astonishing argument that "relational neuroscience has also shown that when we are cut off from others . . . neural pathways suffer. The result is a neurological cascade that can result in chronic irritability and anger, depression, addiction, and chronic physical illness."[11]

I wasn't alone with that experience of loneliness that day in the burgundy minivan on that neighborhood road. And I wasn't alone in the resulting bad moods accompanying those feelings. I realized that when I was most angry, depressed, or acting addicted to food, television, or shopping, I might have stopped and said, "Wait! I'm not really angry, I'm *lonely.*" Or, "I'm not really hungry, I'm *lonely.*"

These feelings, unfortunately, get worse as we age. Research tells us that loneliness is on the rise and affects nearly 40 percent of the middle-aged population.[12] What happened in the minivan, and how the Holy Spirit prompted me to reframe the truth—moving from that Shadow Narrative to the Savior Story of belonging—is also rooted in science. In clinical studies of loneliness, for example, research tried to change the perception of belonging to help those battling disconnection.[13] Those studying loneliness over a seven-year period showed how addressing *dysfunctional thinking* is the single most effective intervention.

No wonder I felt so good and so connected even though I was still physically alone in the van: I told myself the true story of who I am.

I'm included. I'm included with Christ and other believers all the time, no matter where I am.

I rejoiced that day that this "cognitive restructuring" didn't cost me a fortune in therapy or medication; it didn't require hours of meeting with a psychotherapist to heal. It required an attention to God's Word and telling my Savior Story of inclusion. In research terms, social scientists call what happened how I identified "maladaptive social cognition," or in other words, the incorrect or inaccurate ways we understand ourselves.[14]

It apparently does not matter if you take a lonely person and put them into new social situations. What matters isn't people or social interaction as much as how a *person understands herself.* It could be that distorted thinking—feeling and believing one is lonely—is producing the problem.

Thought distortion can destroy your life. It's part of our fallen condition and our sin nature, but we can begin healing by confession, repentance, and walking in obedience to God's Word about our identity. As I shared in the introduction to this study, cognitive restructuring indeed works to aid happiness, but it doesn't solve the problem of sin and our need for salvation. And it doesn't get to the core of our problem. It doesn't unite us to Jesus Christ—our heart's true longing and true home.

I'm learning as an educator and lover of Jesus and His authoritative Word that teaching people to identify their automatic negative thoughts, or their Shadow Narratives that follow them everywhere they go, and replacing these tales with the Signature Stories—their Savior Stories of identity from Ephesians—does indeed help people heal in profound ways. They find freedom from sinful patterns and experience Jesus afresh. They experience biblical inclusion, acceptance, and increasing joy.

Read Philippians 4:8. How can reflecting on what you know to be true, e.g., your being included in Christ and being part of a community with other Christians, replace your Shadow Narrative of loneliness?

Why do Christians experience a special connection with one another that people who don't know Jesus miss? Talk about what you know about Jesus dwelling within you by the Holy Spirit and the effect that reality has on your connections with other Christians.

WHAT SAVIOR STORIES WILL YOU TELL?

Each new semester at Penn State, just as the crisp morning air and red-tipped oak leaves promise that beautiful Pennsylvania autumn, I invite a new class of writing students to tell me their Signature Story.

The Signature Story, according to a professor of marketing at Stanford (who popularized the concept for the business world), defines this kind of story as "an intriguing, authentic, involving narrative with a strategic message. . . . Signature stories represent a critical asset that can be leveraged over time and which can provide inspiration and direction. . . . The challenges are to find, evaluate, gain exposure for, and give legs to signature stories."[15] I teach my students that the story I'm looking for is *authentic, strategic* (meaning it helps their goals in some way), and serves as *an asset.* I stand in front of them, in a typical brown cardigan, glasses, and thermos of coffee with hazelnut creamer, and ask, "What's the story you tell everyone about your life? What moments shape who you are and what you're doing with your life?"

What's the story you tell about your life? Is it authentic, strategic, and an asset?

They of course use these stories for personal statements for graduate school applications, for their professional portfolios, and for interview settings, but they also need these stories to sustain their sense of identity and calling to their particular career choices.

I sip coffee and wait as they begin to scribble down the moments that reveal who they believe they are. I call out encouragement as they brainstorm, quoting Mary Pipher's words in *Writing to Change the World.*

You have something to say that no one else can say. Your history, your unique sensibilities, your sense of place and your language bestow upon you a singular authority. Who but you can describe the hollyhocks in your grandmother's backyard or the creek outside of town that you fished as a child?[16]

"You have something to say that no one else can say!" I call out. I remind them that, by the end of this unit, they will have a powerful story—one filled with all the skills of storytelling including great characters, tension and mystery, emotion, and a final revelation by the end.

But then I say the words that change everything about this process.

"Make sure you tell the *right story*."

They stare back at me, pencils frozen in midair.

I explain that they may have a story they tell over and over again about who they are and why they do what they do, but it's not the best story. It might be a story that ends without hope and leaves the reader contaminated with a sense of defeat and a lack of meaning.

In the business world, for example, you have to be careful about the story you choose to tell because the Signature Story represents a highly strategic form of communication that shapes and enhances a company brand and provides a "north star" for future direction. Great stories fortify companies so that they thrive, enjoying success, loyalty, and longevity. Think about the Signature Stories you may have heard about Apple—the most recognized brand in the world—that showcase Apple as innovative and creative. Can you see Steve Jobs and Steve Wozniak in that old garage, innovating something amazing?[17] That's the story we're supposed to think of when we think of Apple. Or think about Nike shoes and the story of Phil Knight selling shoes out of his car, or Amazon, Coca-Cola, Disney, or a clothing brand you love. A company's Signature Story organizes all the important data someone needs to know about an organization. This story reveals priorities and core values; it provides inspiration. This is the story others first think about when they think about a company or an individual.

What story about your life do you want people to think of first when they think about you?

Someone who loved well and inspired others to do the same

While the Signature Story has everything to do with marketing and business strategy for branding, it also serves *as a guide for personal growth and insight*. The stories we tell ourselves and others about our lives matter deeply because we live out the narratives we believe are true about us. The stories we tell shape us, for better or for worse.

"What's the right story?" a student finally asks.

"Well," I begin and then take a deep breath. "The stories I hear students tell aren't always Signature Stories. They are more like Shadow Narratives. These stories leave you in a state of disappointment, complaint, defeat, hopelessness, and loneliness. Have you ever met someone who complains all the time? Or who constantly rehashes a particular offense or hurt? Or what about someone who sabotages themselves because they keep telling themselves they'll fail or that they aren't good enough or that they aren't smart enough? Do you know what I mean?"

They nod their heads. They know exactly what I'm talking about.

"Now is the time in your life when you begin to tell healing stories, hopeful stories, and harmonizing stories about your life." I write it on the chalkboard in my crooked script: *Healing. Hopeful. Harmonizing.*

I continue: "A Shadow Narrative is the dark story that runs parallel to the joyful, positive Signature Story and attempts to overtake it, like when the setting sun elongates your shadow as you stand there. That Shadow Narrative is always the dark tale you're tempted to tell about your life. These are always tales of loss and pain, victimization, hopelessness, defeat, loneliness, and disconnection. I see people who stay trapped in the Shadow Narrative all their lives when they could tell a different story about what has happened to them and why. Let the story you tell be a different story—the best story you've ever told—about the person you are and want to be. The right story—like a good verb—can change everything."

You might have been hearing this term "shadow" bounced around lately. In the world of creative writing, the "Shadow Narrative" is like the off-screen story—another story happening alongside the dominant narrative that influences how the character behaves. It's usually a dark and haunting tale.

I'm also drawn to this concept because of the "shadow" from Jungian psychology and, more recently, how Peter Scazzero modernized the idea in *The Emotionally Healthy Leader*. He writes a chapter called "Facing Your Shadow" and explains: "Our shadow is the accumulation of untamed emotions, less than pure motives and thoughts that, while largely unconscious, strongly influence and shape your behaviors. It is the damaged but mostly hidden version of who you are."[18] In psychology, the idea of the "shadow" dates back to Carl Jung. In *The Archetypes and the Collective Unconscious*, Jung claimed, "The shadow personifies everything that the subject refuses to acknowledge about himself and yet is always thrusting itself up him directly or indirectly—for instance inferior traits of character and other incompatible tendencies."[19]

The "shadow," both in narrative theory and research in psychology, sounds much like what Paul describes as the "flesh" or the "old self." It's a story that holds us back from being who we want to be in Christ. It's a narrative we feel trapped in that keeps us in darkness.

Think of Isaiah 59:9 and the state of our lives: "We look for light, but all is darkness; for brightness, but we walk in deep shadows." The Shadow Narrative can also be, therefore, the story of our sin. It's often a story about what we most need to confess in our lives.

If your Signature Story—and now what we'll call the Savior Story—brings the fruit of the Spirit (love, joy, peace, patience, kindness, gentleness, goodness, and self-control), the Shadow Narrative connects you to hatred, despair, anxiety, a demanding spirit, unkindness, harshness, bitterness, and impulsivity. The Shadow Narrative is Satan's lie to you about your experience in life. It's a tale of what's being denied you, of all you cannot have, and of all that's missing. It's a tale that begins, like Satan's question to Eve in paradise, about what you feel God has denied you.

SAVIOR STORIES	SHADOW NARRATIVES
Inspire hope	Keep you wounded
Describe God's healing	Disconnect you from Jesus
Connect you to Jesus	Showcase self apart from Christ
Showcase Jesus	Delight in sin
Recall confession and repentance	Manifest Satan's plan
Manifest God's redemption	Deny or distort the Word
Proclaim the truth of the Word	Bring despair

Through this first week of an overview of Ephesians, you have your first opportunity to consider your Savior Story of inclusion (and write out the Shadow Narrative you tell yourself of loneliness and disconnection). These four questions will end every week of our study:

1. Name your Shadow Narrative.
As you thought about your shadow narratives of disconnection, write for a few minutes about just one dominant story you tell yourself of your isolation and loneliness. Set the scene by describing your surroundings and what you remember about yourself—what you're wearing, what you're doing, and what you're thinking.

2. Compose your Savior Story.

Write down the Savior Story of how you're included. What story can you tell of when you truly experienced being "included in Christ"? I told the story of my minivan encounter with truth, so you can use something everyday like that as a model. Or, if you presently battle loneliness and cannot think of a strong story, what has God has taught you as you read through the book of Ephesians and this overview? Choose one passage of Scripture to reflect on in your Savior Story.

3. How does an "included" person live? How do they act? How do they speak?

Contrast this with how excluded and lonely people live and act.

4. Choose one vivid image to remember that you are included in Christ.

I like to see a mosaic, or the rope coming out from my middle like a tether. What about you? Feel free to draw a picture of this image below. Use colored pencils if you wish. Enjoy this moment of relaxation as you consider your included identity.

CONFESSION, REPENTANCE, AND RENEWAL

Talk to God about the areas of your life where you have fostered disconnection and loneliness. Write down some of the behaviors, words, and attitudes that have resulted from this false belief and confess whatever the Holy Spirit brings to mind. Ask God to help you repent—to move in a different direction toward connection and belonging—and invite Him to renew this area of your life. Perhaps you need to forgive someone (or a group) who you felt excluded you. Perhaps you need to reach out to those you have excluded. State the Bible verse from Ephesians that you chose for your Savior Story, and thank God for His work in your heart.

Jealousy, comparison disconnect me

chosen

Ephesians 1:3–14

"I took you from the ends of the earth,
from its farthest corners I called you.
I said, 'You are my servant';
I have chosen you and have not rejected you.
So do not fear, for I am with you;
do not be dismayed, for I am your God.
I will strengthen you and help you;
I will uphold you with my righteous right hand."

—God's words to His people in Isaiah 41:9–10

"You did not choose me, but I chose you and appointed you
so that you might go and bear fruit—fruit that will last—and so
that whatever you ask in my name the Father will give you."

—Jesus speaking in John 15:16

WEEK 2 | DAY 1

A PICTURE OF GOD CHOOSING YOU

Read Ephesians 1.

What comes to mind when you think of the verb *chose* and the description *chosen*? What's the first image you see?

I'm about to share something with you that might just change your life forever.

What if I told you that God *chose* you for Himself and for a very special and marvelous reason? What if I told you that God *chose* you for your specific roles—as student, wife, mother, friend, neighbor, daughter, or employee? Can you imagine living with the security and freedom to know that you belong to a God who chose you?

Think of the synonyms of that word *chosen*: selected, hand-picked, appointed, favored, elected. In examining the Greek translation of the word *chosen* in Scripture, we find it means that God chose us for Himself, for specific tasks He ordains for our lives, and for specific blessings. We'll study the longer passage of this first chapter of Ephesians, but for now, explore this one powerful verse: "For he chose us in him before the creation of the world . . ." (v. 4)

He *chose* us.

What do you see when you read that sentence?

When I think of that sentence, the images have everything to do with my childhood in the 1980s. Let me take you back to 1984 when the song of the year and best MTV stage performance was "Dancing in the Dark" by Bruce Springsteen.[1] In the music video, a gorgeous and sweaty Bruce (in his blue jeans and white shirt rolled up at the sleeves) reaches down into the audience to pull one lucky girl up on the stage from an audience of thousands. He reaches down that strong hand just as he sings "Hey, Baby!" and he pulls Courteney Cox on the stage to dance with him. The video ends with them dancing together as the camera pulls back to show the enormous crowd.

She was chosen. As a ten-year-old girl, I imagined that chosen feeling was something like when Charlie Bucket tears open that chocolate bar's silver inner wrapping to find the golden ticket in *Willy Wonka and the Chocolate Factory.* The music swells as Charlie holds up the golden ticket. Or maybe it was what Aileen Quinn—a girl from Yardley, Pennsylvania—felt in 1982, when, out of eight thousand girls auditioning for the part of Little Orphan Annie in the upcoming movie, she won the role.[2] *She was chosen.*

I think of the word *chosen*, and I mostly feel jealousy and longing. I also feel anxiety of possible future rejection. I live in the Shadow Narrative of past and future rejection instead of my Savior Story of being chosen. Or sometimes I think about those times when I *was* chosen—awards, college acceptances, jobs, and a marriage proposal—and I realize how all those things I thought would help me feel truly chosen never did. We long so badly for someone to choose us—for whatever our heart most wants—and so many of us live daily in the sorrow of rejection.

Right now in your life, for what or by whom do you most want to be chosen?

I sat at the Chinese restaurant across from an accomplished woman. As we ate our egg rolls in our red booth, we began talking about how God was working in her life. She leaned back and tears filled her eyes as she recounted how a man she liked had chosen another woman to date.

With tears now falling, she explained, "It's just another example of how I'm never chosen. I'm always watching how another woman is chosen for everything—that date, that award, or that great experience. I'm never chosen."

I nodded my head because I knew that story well. What woman among us cannot recount the story of when she wasn't chosen for something—or by someone—she desperately wanted? I kept listening, and I heard the Shadow Narrative overtaking the Savior Story. I could read Satan's script through every word she spoke. Her whole life was a Shadow Narrative of *not being chosen.*

This was the story the world and the enemy were writing of her life, but I knew of a different narrative, a story God was writing. In this story, she's *chosen.* She's picked as the desired, royal, treasured possession of the Greatest King.

Could she ever tell that story? What was that story? It was the very day in the Chinese restaurant that God led me to this first verb in Ephesians.

WEEK 2 | DAY 2

CHOSEN IN AND THROUGH

In the first chapter of Paul's letter to the Ephesians, we find the verb that changes everything about our lives and how we experience Jesus and our roles in life. Some readers might note other verbs in this beautiful passage like blessed, predestined, or lavished, but for this week, I invite you to look carefully at this short verb, *chose.*

As you read the passage below, underline all the verbs, but circle the verb *chose* or *chosen*. Also highlight the words "in" and "through."

> Praise be to the God and Father of our Lord Jesus Christ, who has blessed us in the heavenly realms with every spiritual blessing in Christ. For he chose us in him before the creation of the world to be holy and blameless in his sight. In love he predestined us for adoption to sonship through Jesus Christ, in accordance with his pleasure and will—to the praise of his glorious grace, which he has freely given us in the One he loves. In him we have redemption through his blood, the forgiveness of sins, in accordance with the riches of God's grace that he lavished on us. With all wisdom and understanding, he made known to us the mystery of his will according to his good pleasure, which he purposed in Christ, to be put into effect when the times reach their fulfillment—to bring unity to all things in heaven and on earth under Christ.
>
> In him we were also chosen, having been predestined according to the plan of him who works out everything in conformity with the purpose of his will, in order that we, who were the first to put our hope in Christ, might be for the praise of his glory. And you also were included in Christ when you heard the message of truth, the gospel of your salvation. When you believed, you were marked in him with a seal, the promised Holy Spirit, who is a deposit guaranteeing our inheritance until the redemption of those who are God's possession—to the praise of his glory. (Ephesians 1:3–14)

We could spend years on the truths listed in these verses. It does seem like a lot to manage, but let's work through it. This passage includes several other verbs that all cushion what I think is the "operative" word of this passage. An operative word is the most *significant or essential word* that you see. You might choose another operative word in this passage, but I'll explain why "chose" is the most vital.

As we look at what's happening in this passage, we realize that everything depends upon the fact that God chose us. And everything depends on Jesus Christ. The prepositions *in* and *through* always point to the work of Christ that enables this choosing.

Underline everything God does for us in this passage because we are chosen in and through Him.

You'll find that Jesus is blessing us, adopting us, redeeming us, forgiving us, lavishing us with His grace, revealing mysteries to us, working out our lives according to His plan, allowing us to live for the praise of His glory, and guaranteeing our inheritance in heaven.

The beauty of each of these verbs is astounding, and they all flow from our being chosen. God chose us, and we are now blessed, adopted, redeemed, forgiven, lavished with grace, understanding mysteries, living according to His plan, praising Him, and assured of our heavenly dwelling.

Which verb do you love the most in that list and why?

Don't you love that God chose us to *lavish* His love on us? As an evening activity, right before you go to bed, think of an image to accompany each verb and thank Jesus for His gift to you. When I get ready for bed some nights, I think of the verb "lavished" because I lavish myself with hand cream. I always think of *cream* when

I see that word "lavished"—hand cream, whipped cream, ice cream, any cream. I picture God lavishing His love like lots of swirling whipped cream.

As you think about this God who loves us like this, it raises the question, "Who?" Who is this Choosing God? I'm then wondering how, when, why, where, and even more about the who.

See if you can answer these kinds of questions according to the passage.

Who chose you? What is this Choosing God like?

When did He choose you?

How or by what means did He choose you?

Where do you live as a chosen person?

What's different about chosen people?

Why did He choose you?

Here's a fascinating observation: something's happening in the heavenly realms (v. 3), but everything happening is a past tense verb. We have been blessed already; we are already adopted and enjoying riches already lavished. Yet we also will enjoy an inheritance in the future. So we live in the already/not yet of being chosen.

A DIFFICULT CONCEPT

Tomorrow we'll go into detail of the *why*, that is, what God has chosen us *for*. But at this point, you might have the same questions so many have wondered about, debated, argued over: Does this passage mean that God does not choose some people? Doesn't choosing some mean that some are rejected?

I've spent years trying to understand the more confusing verb in Ephesians 1 that we are *predestined*—meaning God decided beforehand about our salvation. Are some not predestined? Or it could be that this verse is broadly affirming that before the creation of the world Gentiles—not Jews only—were to be included in Christ's salvation; so in that way, Paul is stating that even non-Jews who believe were predestined.

I've seen groups torn apart as they argue about *how* God chooses and *who* He chooses. Scholars who are godly and committed to the Word of God differ on this issue. From what I've learned, God does all these: predestines, has foreknowledge about our salvation, and *also extends salvation to all people who may choose Christ.* As Jesus states, "The Son of Man came to seek and to save the lost" (Luke 19:10). And Paul writes, "God our Savior [wants] all people to be saved and to come to a knowledge of the truth" (1 Tim. 2:3–4).

I have found *Word Studies in the Greek New Testament* as well as the *Biblico-Theological Lexicon of the Greek New Testament* by Hermann Cremer to be helpful in discovering a new way to think about Ephesians 1. Cremer, as quoted by theologian Kenneth Wuest, writes:

> The salvation of Israel was for the purpose of making salvation possible to the other nations. The same usage [of the verb *chose*] applies in the case of individual sinners selected out from amongst mankind. These are selected for the purpose of being channels through which the knowledge of salvation might be brought to the rest of mankind, so that those who put their trust in the Lord Jesus as Savior might be saved. This precludes the idea that those not selected are rejected or refused salvation."[3]

Cremer focuses on those chosen in Ephesians as now being "channels through which the knowledge of salvation might be brought to the rest of mankind." These thoughts of mine, of course, approach deep waters in which I can't fully understand about how God chose you or me, why we chose to respond (did we, or did Jesus compel us?); and what theological position about election and choice brings Jesus more glory and showcases His love and mercy more clearly. I'm not sure. We will not ever be sure until we meet Jesus face to face and ask Him.

Whatever position you embrace about predestination, election, and how God chooses us, you can still enjoy this Bible study as we ask other questions that we all can agree on, no matter what our stance on this difficult doctrine.

What helps me move on in this passage is noting the most important and life-changing question. It's not necessarily *how* all this choosing works theologically; it's this question:

Why did He choose us?

Tomorrow we'll look at seven stunning reasons for God's having chosen us.

SEVEN NEW REALITIES

We ended yesterday asking, *Why* did He choose us? I've been thinking about this question for months. I remember that God chooses us for Himself first. He chose us to be with Him, in His holy and magnificent presence.

Consider Ephesians 1:4 and how God "chose us in him before the creation of the world to be holy and blameless in his sight." That's more important that anything else because it shows the heart of God to desire that we would be "in his sight" and in His presence. He wants to spend time with us. He wants us in His presence. You might also note verse 12 and how we are chosen for the "praise of his glory"— meaning the goal of our lives should be to manifest the power and presence of God, to bear witness to His greatness, in every situation in our lives.

SEVEN REASONS WE'RE CHOSEN

1. God chose us to be His treasured possession.

Read aloud Deuteronomy 14:2, Psalm 135:4, and Malachi 3:17. Each passage showcases that God sees us as His "treasured possession." We are also, according to Isaiah 62:3, "a crown of splendor in the LORD's hand, a royal diadem in the hand of [our] God."

Do you wake up and feel like a treasured possession and a rare, exotic jewel? Do you walk around your house and workplace and behave with the confidence and joy inside that you are God's rare and precious treasure?

How would life change for you if you did? Journal your thoughts.

2. God chose us to *belong to Him as a child* in a new household.

God chooses to make us "fellow citizens with God's people and also members of God's household." We are chosen to join a new household, with new brothers and sisters, who together become the family of God. Most importantly, this family has a loving Father who chose us to belong and who assures us of "his eternal fatherly care and provision, a love and indulgence that exceeds our imagination."[4] He meets our every need because we are His beloved, much-loved children.

Imagine being chosen to join a perfect, loving household. What is this family like? Write down some of the characteristics of the most amazing family you can imagine.

3. God chose us *to worship Him.*

We are not just chosen as God's treasured possession and to join His family, we are also chosen to then praise Him. First Peter 2:9 beautifully states the intention of our chosen status. Peter writes, "But you are a chosen people, a royal priesthood, a holy nation, God's special possession, that you may declare the praises of him who called you out of darkness into his wonderful light."

We were made *to declare the praises* of God. In whatever situation God chooses to place us, we're chosen to worship Him in the midst of those circumstances. Can you imagine facing some difficult thing and asking first, "How can I worship God in this? If I truly believe I'm chosen for this situation, what would it mean to declare His praises in this pain, disappointment, confusion, or loss?" Can you "give thanks in all circumstances; for this is God's will for you in Christ Jesus" (1 Thess. 5:18)? Worshiping Jesus by giving thanks for His power, goodness, sufficiency, mercy, beauty, and love for me—no matter what—is part of my chosen identity.

What does it mean to worship Jesus in every situation? How would someone be able to do this? If you felt chosen right now—in whatever difficult situation you're in—to "declare the praises of God" and to "give thanks," how would that change your perspective?

4. God chose us *to be conformed* to His image.

Perhaps you still wonder, "Why did God choose me? For what purpose beyond belonging to Him as His treasured possession, joining a new household called the family of God, and praising and worshiping Him?" We find in Paul's letter to the Romans (8:29) another profound statement: "For God . . . *chose them* to become like his Son" (NLT, emphasis mine). God chose us to become like Jesus and to allow Christ to form Himself within our very souls (Gal. 4:19) so that we radiate His presence.

Think about 2 Corinthians 2:14: "But thanks be to God, who always leads us as captives in Christ's triumphal procession and uses us to spread the aroma of the knowledge of him everywhere." Our lives also will manifest in increasing measure the fruits of the Spirit of Galatians 5:22–23: love, joy, peace, patience, kindness, goodness, gentleness, faithfulness, and self-control. God chose us to live lives that display Jesus to the world through these attitudes that accompany Spirit-led and Spirit-empowered actions to bless the world.

What does the phrase "conformed to the image of Christ" mean to you?

Biblical maturity means responding as Jesus would in every situation. What do you think this could look like in your life?

5. God chose us to *display His power* and splendor in our lives.

In addition to displaying God's character as we live conformed to the image of Christ, God chooses us to manifest *His power and His glory.* Some translations of the Bible use the phrase "display [His] splendor" like in Isaiah 60:21 where God calls us the "work of [His] hands, for the display of [His] splendor." I love the word "splendor" because we don't hear it much in common speech, but it means absolute magnificence, beauty, grandeur, and opulence. It's an over-the-top kind of word.

When God chooses us as His own, He desires to showcase His splendor through our lives. Can you believe that? How incredible to think that God wants to reveal His power, presence, and glory through our ordinary lives! When we face a difficult circumstance, consider that God may have brought you to that place in order to display His power there.

He wants to make our lives so beautiful and joyful in the midst of difficulty that people who look at us would note the presence of Jesus Christ. It excites me so much to consider that God desires to display Himself through us to the world. He chose us to make His name famous, and I pray along with Isaiah 26:8: "Your name and renown are the desire of our hearts."

Write down a time when you believe God was showcasing His power and presence through your life.

Think about your current life's challenges. Imagine that God brought you to this situation in order to display His power right there.

6. God chose us to *do good works*.

God gave us a marvelous life purpose when He chose us. John 15 teaches us about our bearing fruit as we stay connected to Him. Jesus says in John 15:16, "I chose you and appointed you so that you might go and bear fruit—fruit that will last—and so that whatever you ask in my name the Father will give you." Jesus also says in Matthew 4:19, "Come follow me . . . and I will send you out to fish for people."

The sense of being chosen by God to fish for people—and that we are chosen and appointed for this—all made sense when I read 2 Corinthians 5:18–20. Even though I was a graduate student earning a PhD with dreams of becoming a professor, I knew that alongside this goal, God had a grander mission for me. Paul writes, "All this is from God, who reconciled us to himself through Christ and gave us the ministry of reconciliation: that God was reconciling the world to himself in Christ, not counting people's sins against them. And he has committed to us the message of reconciliation. We are therefore Christ's ambassadors, as though God were making his appeal through us." I realized that every situation for which God chose me (living with my roommates, teaching classes, sitting in graduate seminars) was an invitation to serve as an ambassador.

In every situation, I was chosen and appointed to bear fruit—as are you as a Christ follower. When we're confused about what to do or feeling like we don't belong somewhere, we can remember that we have been chosen and appointed as an ambassador in that place.

When I realized this truth during that season of life, each day took on supernatural purpose and meaning, and my whole life changed to align myself to God's choosing and appointing me to bear fruit. My plans and great goals still came about—including earning the PhD, teaching, speaking, and writing—but instead of living for my own glory and plans, I submitted them to Jesus and knew His beautiful and powerful will in choosing me: to bear fruit for Him.

We can think carefully about Ephesians 2:10. Remind yourself that *I was "created in Christ Jesus to do good works, which God prepared in advance for [me] to do."* Wake up each new day to live as a fisherman and ambassador and to complete the good works God prepared in advance for you to do.

How would your day change if you believed God chose you and appointed you to bear fruit where He has placed you?

What if your life today is all about God positioning you to be an ambassador, even if you don't like your schedule?

7. God chose us to *live differently* from the rest of the world.

In John 15:19, Jesus states another reason for His choosing us. He says, "You do not belong to the world, but I have chosen you out of the world." If you match this verse with Paul's explanation in Romans 12:2, you can understand what it means to be chosen "out of the world." Paul writes, "Do not conform to the pattern of this world, but be transformed by the renewing of your mind."

For the last two decades, Jesus has been teaching me through His Word what the "pattern of this world" could mean. I think about the focus on physical appearance, the accumulation of wealth, and the desire for fame and prestige. I think about greed and selfish ambition. I think about the pursuit of pleasure and happiness as our culture's highest values.

Chosen people live differently, and as we move on in our study of the next verb in Ephesians, you'll learn more about what it means to live "out of this world."

What do you think the "pattern of this world" means?

How can knowing God chose you "out of the world" help you live differently?

GOD CHOSE US IN EVERY SITUATION:

- To belong to Him as His treasured possession

- To join a new household

- To worship Him

- To conform to the image of Jesus Christ

- To display His power and splendor

- To complete the good works He has planned

- To live differently from the rest of the world

WEEK 2 | DAY 4

WHEN YOU'RE NOT CHOSEN

The verb *chose* from Ephesians 1:3–14 shows us a powerful new identity. We are *chosen people,* and chosen people live as if we are a treasured possession, part of a royal household, as worshipers conformed to the image of Christ and displaying the splendor of God, as ready to complete the good works set apart for us, and according to a new, biblical pattern of life. I love to make compare/contrast charts to help me understand my new identity in Christ. Think about the seven realities of your *chosen* identity:

CHOSEN PEOPLE ARE	
Treasured	instead of worthless and rejected
Part of a new family	instead of lonely and abandoned
Worshiping God	instead of worshiping self or idols
Becoming more like Christ	instead of increasing in ungodliness
Displaying God's power and splendor	instead of living ordinary and self-empowered
Set apart for good works	instead of striving for achievement
Living according to a new pattern	instead of conforming to the culture

The Puritan preacher Jonathan Edwards sums up our being chosen in a sermon delivered in the eighteenth century. He proclaims:

God has chosen you not merely to be his subjects and servants, but to be his children, to be his particular treasure. He has chosen you to be blessed forever in the enjoyment of himself, and to dwell with him in his glory. He has given you from all eternity to his Son, to be united unto him, to become the spouse of Christ. He has chosen you that you might be holy and without blame, that you might have your filth taken away, and that you might have the image of God put upon you, and that your soul might be adorned, to be the bride of his glorious and dear Son. What cause for love is here![5]

When we consider this great love of God and the privileges of living as His chosen sons and daughters, why do you think it's so difficult to live from this chosen reality? Theologian Eugene Peterson explains one reason why. He writes,

> Everybody I have ever become acquainted with has a story, usually from childhood, of not being chosen: not chosen for the glee club, not chosen for the basketball team, the last chosen in a neighborhood sandlot softball team (which is worse than not being chosen at all), not chosen for a job, not chosen as a spouse. Not chosen carries the blunt messages that I have no worth, that I am not useful, that I am good for nothing.[6]

Peterson further explains that when we don't live from the reality of our being chosen from Ephesians, we do anything to become noticed and to ease the pain of our story of not being chosen.

What realities of your being chosen are most meaningful to you? Are there any on the list above you doubt, or struggle with?

As I looked more deeply into the brain science behind rejection, it made perfect sense that my friend in the Chinese restaurant (Day One of this week) interpreted her life through the lens of rejection. In fact, people who experience rejection often misread social situations and look for clues, real and imagined, to confirm exclusion and judgment. They choose to believe that everyone dislikes them and wants to reject them.

They become "rejection sensitive" and examine their environment—and then avoid social situations—to protect themselves from the possible pain of rejection.[7] And this is *actual pain* they seek to avoid; research recently discovered that when we experience rejection, we activate the same neural pathways as one experiencing physical pain.[8] Rejection, researchers claim, is often worse than physical pain because, unlike physical pain where we can't remember the actual pain, we relive the memories of rejection acutely.

We adjust our entire lives to protect against this pain of rejection. Perhaps we don't apply for certain jobs, date certain people, or attempt something new in public because we fear this experience of rejection. As a result, our loneliness and disconnection increase.

We live from rejection and not God's choosing of us.

Is it possible to intervene in this story and change the story of our rejection?

FEATURED SAVIOR STORY

My daughter Sarah—who gives full permission to bless you with this story—experienced such a painful rejection in sixth grade that its results led to a form of anxiety and fear that sent our whole family into a tailspin. Her best friend rejected her, choosing the popular crowd and avoiding her at lunch. Sarah ate lunch alone in the art room for months and would come home crying and sick to her stomach over being rejected.

To make matters worse, a popular group of girls expressed to Sarah how awkward she was socially. This experience marked my daughter in such a way that every social interaction generated profound insecurity. Was she being awkward again? Was she annoying people? And if a person did show interest in friendship, Sarah often said, "Does she like me, I mean really like me like a true friend, or will she change her mind? How do I know? Will she reject me later?"

For the three years of middle school, we worked on Sarah's internal Savior Story of who she was, and how even though she had no seat in the lunchroom she was "seated with Christ" at the Greatest Table with the Greatest King in the heavenly realms. (We'll talk about this in the next chapter of Ephesians.)

We also wrote a family motto that "every rejection is God's protection." This made the rejection not about Sarah, but about God's sovereignty and love for her life. As the years went on, that group that rejected Sarah became hurtful, depressed, and miserable. And the former best friend returned to Sarah, apologizing about this colossal mistake in choosing the popular crowd over her.

Even though Sarah accepted her apology and truly reconciled, the damage was so deep that it colored how Sarah experienced her life as she entered into high school. She had to actively fight the lie that she would be rejected. She had to actively choose not to live in that Shadow Narrative of rejection and live the Savior Story that God had never rejected her, that He was in control of her life, and that her unique and quirky personality was a gift for the world.

She changed the narrative and saw the rejection she had experienced in middle school through the lens of protection and provision. She rewrote the story that God chose her, that God was seated with her, and that she didn't have to live a life of rejection. She learned Psalm 94:14 (NLT): "The LORD will not reject his people; he will not abandon his special possession." She could also see that God chose her for other friends and different experiences. Mostly, she learned the spiritual truth that God chose her.

He chose her. He chose her for Himself.

I consulted a family life coach to help us navigate what we were experiencing regarding Sarah's understanding of social rejection. The coach helped us understand the importance of building Sarah's confidence again—of helping her see the gifts God had given her and the talents she was developing. I would say over and over again to Sarah, "You are a gift to the world. You are a joy to be around. You bring joy wherever you go. You are chosen as God's precious treasure. Jesus and others choose to be with you. You are chosen."

Around this time, a group of girls from a teen Bible study over a thousand miles away in Texas heard the story of Sarah's middle school rejection from their leader who knew our family. One day, a package arrived filled with letters written from these girls to encourage Sarah. Sarah sat on her bed and cried as letter after letter fell into her lap from teens she had never met—and had nothing in common with—other than they loved Jesus too and wanted her to know she wasn't alone.

I went into the bathroom and cried. Five years later, Sarah still reads those letters before she goes to bed some nights. She knows she's included with those girls and chosen *to belong to the family of God. I think in heaven they'll all have a seat in the lunch-room together.*

This is the story I want her life to tell.

Most likely, we can each recall a filmstrip of rejection: of not being chosen, of being ignored, passed over, of always being pushed to the background while some other girl was chosen. Or, maybe you don't struggle with any vivid memories of re-jection, but you do feel invisible, like nobody would notice, much less *choose*, you. My teenage daughters tell me how, right now, they experience how God has cho-sen them; they do feel special to God, loved by God, and seen by God. I want to remind them of this matchless chosen reality every day of their lives. I want them to store it up deep inside of them—the way I store away dried tomatoes or sauces or summer raspberries to bring them out during the cold, bitter winter when the Pennsylvania landscape is so stark it's nearly impossible to remember that anything once grew so beautifully there.

I want them to store up stories of feeling chosen because I know what's coming: I know that as they begin dating, applying for colleges, internships, graduate schools and then jobs, to desire marriage and, perhaps, families of their own, that it's not always going to feel like they are chosen. I've journeyed alongside so many women who live in the daily agony of *not being chosen.*

It's unimaginably painful to wait on the Lord for the experiences and people we most desire—including marriage partners, children, and dream schools or jobs—because we often begin to live in the Shadow Narrative, like my friend in the Chinese restaurant, of never being chosen.

So we slowly, subtly, and often unconsciously begin to say to ourselves:

That's me. Always rejected. Never chosen. It's always the other girl. It's never me.

But we can change our narrative.

My story of being chosen actually began as a twelve-year-old in my bedroom. I remember crying out to Jesus to forgive me of my sin and rescue me. I knew I was His chosen and valued child that day. I knew He could see me and would take care of me.

Another chapter in my new story came when I was reeling from the pain of a high school boyfriend who left for college while I finished my senior year. As the story goes, he found someone new and fell in love with her. The first heartbreak crushed me so deeply it felt like I'd been dragged to a new territory of sadness and rejection. The worthless feelings began to weave that Shadow Narrative that *I wasn't chosen*. She was chosen. In such pain over the loss, I eventually attended the same college as this boy I pined for. Watching him and his new girlfriend together made me physically and mentally sick.

But God was pursuing me that year at the University of Virginia. As I read my childhood Bible in my dorm room that year, Jesus met me in such a powerful way that, even though my boyfriend rejected me, I discovered I was still cherished and chosen.

I read John 10:10 (NASB) where Jesus says, "I came that [you] may have life, and have it abundantly." My journal from that year features these phrases from Psalm 73:25–26: "Whom have I in heaven but you? And earth has nothing I desire besides you. My flesh and my heart may fail, but God is the strength of my heart and my portion forever."

I also wrote down and memorized Jeremiah 29:11: "'For I know the plans I have for you,' declares the LORD, 'plans to prosper you and not to harm you, plans to give you hope and a future.'" And I began to rewrite my story.

Remember the image of Bruce Springsteen's hand reaching down to choose that one girl to come up on the stage to dance? Well, when I was beginning to believe that God chose me for Himself and for a special future, God led me to a verse that still brings me to tears. It's from Psalm 18:16: "He reached down from on high and took hold of me; he drew me out of deep waters." God was reaching down with His mighty hand, choosing me for Himself.

Knowing you are chosen—changing that Shadow Narrative—isn't something that you decide once and then move on; instead, we need to remind ourselves of the truth of it in each new season of life.

Do you have a tangible reminder—such as Sarah's letters from Texas—that God has chosen you for Himself and for a special future? If you can't think of something, use the image of God's reaching down from on high (or a hand reaching from the stage) and taking hold of you; how do you respond to this image of Him?

I began to write afresh my Savior Story of God choosing me the day my friend Crystal in Texas (Texan women are always blessings to me—what is it about Texans?) called me when I battled enormous insecurity about the task of raising my daughters. I felt like a failure every day. I had no idea what I was doing, and at my worst, I imagined my children would do much better in life if God brought them another mother instead. I even wondered if my husband would do much better with another wife. And even God would do better with another kind of Christian than someone so messed up inside as I was in my twenties and thirties.

Crystal said this: "Heather, God chose you to be the mother of those girls. And so, therefore, you are the perfect mother for them."

Me? Perfect for them? Perfect in my non-fashion sense, obsession with grammar and vivid verbs, lack of knowledge of anything musical or mathematical, awkward social interactions, and over-the-top energy? Me?

I began to love motherhood that day when I believed God chose me for my children. I began to love marriage on the day I realized that I'm the best wife for this man. And, most importantly, I believed that God chose me for Himself and the tasks He appoints, and I'm perfect because Jesus makes me perfect.

Oh, what a change it makes to know I'm chosen!

And, on a practical mothering note, understanding that God chose you as His special, prized, favored possession isn't just a theological nicety. It's a reality that even a young child can carry in her heart. Yesterday, my younger daughter recounted a day chock full of rejection and exclusion. Her poster didn't win the poster contest; another girl's was chosen. Her essay wasn't chosen for the group that could move on to a special class for talented writers; other pupils' writings were chosen. Her friends chose other, more popular girls for their lunch table; my daughter feels invisible, rejected, *not chosen*. And all this happens by 11:45 a.m. In the afternoon, she's not chosen for the prized solo spots for the concert. The list goes on.

We're walking and talking by lantern light through our neighborhood. The silvery moonlight falls upon the slick autumn leaves. The acorns crunch beneath our feet as we pass by home after home glowing from within as a hundred other families are enjoying the benefits of a different kind of day. My daughter wonders aloud what other girls must experience and how she alone suffers.

Kate turns her little face up to mine. She's lit by moonlight and her cheeks show the pink flush of the cold evening. "Mom, I did remember what you told me about being chosen by God. I did remember that. And I prayed to Him during my day. I know I'm chosen by *Him* when everyone else is chosen for all the prizes."

We walk on, *chosen.*

Begin taking notes regarding your "filmstrip of rejection."

What current life roles and circumstances generate the most insecurity for you? How might you live freely from insecurity, jealousy, and comparison as you think about God choosing you and designating you specifically for all the roles and tasks in your life?

WEEK 2 | DAY 5

WRITING YOUR STORIES

One day, we'll inhabit our chosen identity in its fullest sense—when Jesus welcomes us into His glorious kingdom and says, "Well done, my good and faithful servant." Imagine the angels. Picture the crowns given us that we then lay at His feet. Imagine all of us there together, worshiping. Envision golden light and beauty too magnificent for the imagination to summon.

Imagine you and Jesus reviewing the pictures of your *chosen* story and how you'll laugh and cry together over various scenes, painful and joyous. But right now, I pray we know Jesus better and better as the God who chooses us. And I remember Paul's prayer for us after he outlines our chosen identity. He next writes:

> I keep asking that the God of our Lord Jesus Christ, the glorious Father, may give you the Spirit of wisdom and revelation, so that you may know him better. I pray that the eyes of your heart may be enlightened in order that you may know the hope to which he has called you, the riches of his glorious inheritance in his holy people, and his incomparably great power for us who believe. (Ephesians 1:17–19)

Chosen people, as you have now prayed along with Paul, can know Jesus by that incomparable Spirit of wisdom and revelation. Chosen people live enlightened to hope, riches, and power. Chosen people are filled in every way with the fullness of Jesus Christ.

So now I invite you to walk on, *chosen.*

1. Name your Shadow Narratives.

Part One: What story do you tell yourself over and over again of rejection and not being chosen?

Part Two: You might instead have stories in your heart where you felt so loved and chosen, and you hold on to these as very important to your identity. List examples from the past that comprise what it means that you feel chosen. Why do you think these experiences cannot compare to what Jesus offers you in being chosen by Him?

Part Three: Do you have a secret fantasy story of what it would mean that you were chosen? In ministry, I've met with married women who live out a fantasy life in which they picture an old boyfriend returning to choose them—and their marriage suffers. I say, "This is the Shadow Narrative that's a dark, poisonous lie." I've met with single women who cultivate such a vivid fantasy life that they spend hours alone in the bedroom living out a fantasy dating relationship. You aren't alone if you need to confess the Shadow Narrative of fantasy.

2. Compose your Savior Story of being God's chosen.

What was happening in your life before you understood what it meant to become a Christian?

How did you come to understand your sin and need for a Savior?

What does it mean to you (in the past or right now) that God chose you for Himself?

3. How do you as a chosen person now live? Compare the old, rejected you to the new, chosen you. Consult the seven ways chosen people live listed in Day Three.

4. Choose an image or object to remind you that you are God's chosen.

Is it a piece of jewelry to remind yourself that you are a rare jewel? Do you picture God's hand reaching down to choose you (like Bruce Springsteen)? Maybe you think of chocolate like Charlie Bucket winning the golden ticket or a spotlight on you and Jesus.

CONFESSION, REPENTANCE, AND RENEWAL

As we close our study of the verb *chosen,* you might feel inspired but also discouraged. Perhaps you believe that your Shadow Narrative is too strong and that you'll never understand how to live in light of Ephesians 1. In the Christian life, I'm learning that all growth in Jesus happens through confession (agreeing with God about our sin), repentance (choosing to turn from our sin and go in a different direction), and renewal (asking the Holy Spirit to help us grow in this area so we are renewed in our minds).

One way to think about sin is *going our own independent way from God.* For this chapter of our study, we can confess to God that we have sinned against Him by choosing to live in rejection and pain and perhaps a lack of forgiveness or bitterness. We can confess our fantasy life. We can confess our unbelief and even our idolatry that we have been longing to be chosen by a person or group other than Jesus to meet our needs.

We can finally confess all the ways we aren't living in our chosen identity, living instead from the pattern of the world. The Holy Spirit—who guides us in all truth—will show you those areas of your life that are out of alignment with God's Word.

First John 1:9 says this: "If we confess our sins, he is faithful and just and will forgive us our sins and purify us from all unrighteousness." This is a wonderful promise that Jesus not only forgives us, but He also cleanses and purifies us. You can trust Jesus to help you fully embrace and inhabit your new identity as chosen in Christ.

After you write out a confession to Jesus, you can read Hosea 14:4 where God declares: "I will heal their waywardness and love them freely, for my anger has turned away from them."

seated

Ephesians 2:1–10

"All seats provide equal viewing of the universe."

—Museum Guide at the Hayden Planetarium

THE SAVIOR STORY OF SEATED

Read Ephesians 2

If I could choose only *one portion* of the Bible that has changed me more powerfully, more completely, and more radically than any other passage in Scripture, it would be Ephesians 2:1–10. In fact, one verse in Ephesians 2 became such a powerful Savior Story for me that it led to a book contract,[1] speaking engagements, interviews, and many professional opportunities including more books and now, this very study you hold in your hands.

I recently showed my students a statement from motivational speaker Doug Stevenson, the founder of Story Theater International, to inspire them as they compose their Signature Stories. Stevenson writes, "A signature story is a story that you become known for, maybe even famous for. Over time, you become so good at performing this story that people ask for it again and again. I know speakers that have made over a million dollars with one good story."[2]

I never set out to make millions or become famous with my story of Ephesians 2:6, but I tell my students about the power of writing a story that "you become known for" that will help people so they want to hear you tell it again and again. I wrote a book about my story of Ephesians 2:6, and this Savior Story became the most important story of my life and the one people often associate with me.

And God is writing a story in your heart, too—one just as powerful and transformative as mine. He's writing your Savior Story, and I cannot wait for you to tell it.

But first, let me tell you my Savior Story of Ephesians 2:6.

A lightning bolt of realization hit me on a summer day in late July as I read Ephesians 2. There I sat, reading the words I'd read a hundred times before. Only this time, the Holy Spirit used a single verb to change everything about me. It was the simple verb *seated* that you'll find in verse 6. As I read the entire passage, I said this: "I'm seated with Christ. But I'm not living like I have a seat at the Greatest Table with the Greatest King. I'm living like someone fighting for a seat at the table."

Everything about my life was a fight for an invitation to the seat I thought would finally bring me life and happiness and love and belonging. I thought that if only I could have a seat with the thin and beautiful, rich and famous, or accomplished and prestigious people, then life would really begin for me. I lived all day long like something was missing because I was waiting for a seat at the table.

And then I read Ephesians 2:6. I'm already seated with Christ.

As you read the following ten verses, underline all the actions that God takes in this passage. Circle the verb "seated" when you finish.

As for you, you were dead in your transgressions and sins, in which you used to live when you followed the ways of this world and of the ruler of the kingdom of the air, the spirit who is now at work in those who are disobedient. All of us also lived among them at one time, gratifying the cravings of our flesh and following its desires and thoughts. Like the rest, we were by nature deserving of wrath.

But because of his great love for us, God, who is rich in mercy, made us alive with Christ even when we were dead in transgressions—it is by grace you have been saved. And God raised us up with Christ and seated us with him in the heavenly realms in Christ Jesus, in order that in the coming ages he might show the incomparable riches of his grace, expressed in his kindness to us in Christ Jesus.

For it is by grace you have been saved, through faith—and this is not from yourselves, it is the gift of God—not by works, so that no one can boast. For we are God's handiwork, created in Christ Jesus to do good works, which God prepared in advance for us to do. (Ephesians 2:1–10)

I love Ephesians 2:1–10 because Paul outlines a way of thinking and learning. He showcases the Shadow Narrative:

> As for you, you were dead.
> You were following the devil.
> You were enslaved to ungodly desires and thoughts.

Think about those phrases for a moment and write down some characteristics of people who live like this. Before Christ rescued us we were:

dead in transgressions and sins   **What is this like?**

following the ruler of the kingdom of the air   **What is this like?**

Glorifying un Godly things

gratifying the desires of the flesh and the mind   **What is this like?**

selfishness

What a terrible description of a life apart from Christ! What's so beautiful about this passage in Ephesians is the way Paul sets up the contrast of a new life in Christ. Instead of being dead, God made us alive and seated us with Him. Instead of following Satan, we now belong to Jesus and carry out the good works God prepared beforehand for us. When Paul illuminates the Savior Story that God—this merciful, loving, and gracious God—*makes us alive* in Christ together, *seats* us with Christ, and *prepares* good works for our lives, he shows us an entirely new way to live.

Fill out this chart:

NEW LIFE IN CHRIST	WHAT DOES THIS MEAN TO YOU?
Made us alive	*Given purpose and meaning in Jesus*
Raised us up and seated us	*Given us a place at the table*
Created to do good works	*Given opportunity to show examples of Gods love*

As I looked carefully at this passage in Ephesians 2, I noted the operative verb "seated." That little verb caught me off guard. I could understand that I was now spiritually alive and enjoying Jesus and that He had good works prepared in advance for me to do.

But what could it mean that I was seated with Christ? It is a past tense verb, meaning that this seated reality *has already happened to* us. I pictured the Knights of the Round Table invited by King Arthur to take their seats. I pictured myself as Guinevere in a beautiful gown. How would I live differently if I really believed I had a seat at the Greatest Table with the Greatest King?

I knew it so strongly: My Shadow Narrative was one of always being excluded, of longing for that special invitation to the seat and the table that would finally bring me life. I lived in depression, anxiety, comparison, and jealousy all day long. But as I read Ephesians 2:6 on that summer day, the Holy Spirit brought the deepest revelation of my life besides knowing Jesus as my Savior: I was already seated at the table my heart most desired. Everything I longed for in my life was already happening because I was with Jesus in the seat I'd been longing for my whole life.

That day, I began to ask myself how people seated with Christ truly live. I began to wonder how to picture this seat in the heavenly realms with as much clarity as Paul—who wrote Ephesians while under house arrest in Rome—held it in his mind to proclaim he was seated in that place of royalty despite his circumstances.

JESUS IS SEATED

We know that the apostle Paul went through many hardships (e.g., see 2 Cor. 11:23–28). And yet, he knew how to be content (Phil. 4:12). How could this be? It was because of whatever situation or "seat" he found himself in, his life was elsewhere, in another seat.

> Since, then, you have been raised with Christ, set your hearts on things above, where Christ is, seated at the right hand of God. Set your minds on things above, not on earthly things. For you died, and your life is now hidden with Christ in God. When Christ, who is your life, appears, then you also will appear with him in glory. (Colossians 3:1–4)

This seat with Christ captured Paul's heart and mind, and he chose, in even the direst circumstances, to celebrate how he had been "raised with Christ" and was now seated with Him in the heavenly realms.

Can you imagine knowing that you are seated at a royal table in the heavenly realms no matter what's actually happening in your physical experience? Paul did this, and so can I. And so can you. Do the implications take your breath away?

I began to research what made this experience of being "seated" so profound to Paul, and learned something even more beautiful. When you read in Ephesians 2 that we are raised "with" Christ and seated "in" Him, you must turn to Hebrews 10 and take a step back. You must ask yourself why it is so important that Jesus Christ himself is "seated." Here is where I cover my face with my hands and close my eyes in wonder.

We know from Jewish law concerning the administration and service in the temple that Jewish priests were not allowed to *sit down*. They always stood. In fact, the tabernacle had no seats.[3] We read in Hebrews 10:11–14 this incredible fact about Jesus:

Day after day every priest stands and performs his religious duties; again and again he offers the same sacrifices, which can never take away sins. But when this priest [Jesus] had offered for all time one sacrifice for sins, he sat down at the right hand of God. . . . For by one sacrifice he has made perfect forever those who are being made holy.

The high priest *does not sit down*, yet here, Jesus, our High Priest forever, *sits down*. What can this mean? When I compare the verbs *stand* and *sit* in this passage, I begin to wonder what made the verb "sit" so remarkable to the audience. I found a fascinating answer in a nineteenth-century sermon. On February 4, 1872, the British preacher Charles Spurgeon delivered a sermon on Hebrews 10 called, "The Only Atoning Priest." We read the following:

> The priests stood because there was work to do; still must they present their sacrifices; but our Lord sits down because there is no more sacrificial work to do; atonement is complete, he has finished his task. There were no seats in the tabernacle. Observe the Levitical descriptions and you will see that there were no resting-places for the priests in the holy place. Not only were none allowed to sit, but there was nothing whatever to sit upon. . . . A priest never sat in the tabernacle, he was under a dispensation which did not afford rest, and was not intended to give it, a covenant of works which gives the soul no repose. Jesus sits in the holy of holies, and herein we see that his work is finished.[4]

Spurgeon's commentary on Hebrews 10 makes Ephesians 2:6 come alive even more. Jesus "sat down at the right hand of God" having finished, once and for all, the sacrifice for sin.

It is finished.

No sacrifice for sin—past, present, and future sin—is needed. If I were with you right now in a Bible study setting, I would say: "Turn to the person beside you and explain in your own words why it matters that Jesus is seated." It's the most profound concept and so theologically stirring that I could spend the whole Bible study just talking about Jesus' work on the cross.

So take a moment and explain in your own words why it matters that Jesus is seated.

He has completed his sacrifice for our sin

Jesus finished the work of the priests. He is the High Priest who takes away the sins of the world, and He invites you and me to take our seat in the heavenly realms beside Him.

We can sit down. In fact, we *are* sitting down. We have been raised with Christ, who has "seated us" in the heavenly realms.

It's a past tense verb.

It suggests something has already happened to us.

We've already been seated in the heavenly realms, yet here we remain in a physical body in a material world. Paul often put theological truths in the past tense in order to affirm the certainty of them happening at a future date, and he maintained the same simultaneity that we feel when we read this verb. It's a both now-and-not-yet kind of verb, just like when Jesus claims the "kingdom of God is in your midst" in Luke 17:21.

We know that we will enter into heaven when we physically die, but there's also a sense that some part of the kingdom of heaven has already begun in us *right now*. The kingdom of God, like our seat in the heavenly realms, will come about in fullness as we enter heaven, but as believers, we are at this very moment part of God's kingdom and seated with Christ.

In Ephesians 2, most biblical scholars I've read believe that Paul's statement announces something true about us *in the present moment*. As I read Ephesians 2:6 in context, I find more evidence for this.

Circle every word that is in the past (or has already been done for us).

> As for you, you were dead in your transgressions and sins. . . . But because of his great love for us, God, who is rich in mercy, made us alive with Christ even when we were dead in transgressions—it is by grace you have been saved. And God raised us up with Christ and seated us with him in the heavenly realms in Christ Jesus, in order that in the coming ages he might show the incomparable riches of his grace, expressed in his kindness to us in Christ Jesus. For it is by grace you have been saved, through faith—and this is not from yourselves, it is the gift of God—not by works, so that no one can boast. For we are God's handiwork, created in Christ Jesus to do good works, which God prepared in advance for us to do. (vv. 1, 4–10)

Here, Paul talks about how we have *already been saved* and that we have *already been made alive with Christ*. This has already happened. So why would it not follow that his next statement reveals an equally accomplished reality? We *have been seated* in Christ in the heavenly realms. If this is something happening right now in the heavenly realms, and not at some future date, then what would it look like to add this verb to my arsenal of theological terms?

As we asked regarding *chosen*, let's fill out this list of questions to ground us in our understanding. These are the same questions that made me so excited to embrace this new identity.

Who seats us?

God

Where are we seated?

At table with Christ – heavenly realm

When are we seated?

now & forever

How are we seated?

next to Christ

Why or for what purpose are we seated?

show the riches of his grace

The hardest question for me to answer was the "where," since we are seated "in the heavenly realms." I wanted to somehow picture this reality since it seemed so abstract. I have a picture and a mood in my mind when I read the word "seated." Just like for *chosen* and how I see God's hand reaching down from on high to take hold of me, I see myself in Ephesians 2 as called by a Great King to my seat at the Greatest Table.

Do you see yourself as seated? Tomorrow you'll have a chance to describe that seat.

IMAGINE YOUR SEAT

Can you see yourself called to your seat? In my imagination, it plays out like Arthurian legend and the famed Round Table.[5] I see a great round table, fit for the greatest knights of Camelot.

I know it's rather old-fashioned, and maybe the only image you have in your mind is Disney's 1963 animated classic *The Sword in the Stone* when you hear about King Arthur. Maybe you have vague memories of these Arthurian legends from history class when you studied the medieval period and this legendary fifth-century British king. I'm not sure what you see in your mind, but I'll share what I imagine.

I picture King Arthur calling the knights of Camelot to the Round Table. If you remember, at the Round Table, nobody is inferior or superior to anyone else. King Arthur chose a round table for this very purpose: to settle disputes over superiority. Every knight was equal at the Round Table. In my mind, I see the knights take their seats. Each one has his own place, his own talents, and his own assignments. They sit battle ready, uniquely equipped, devoted to the kingdom, and interdependent.

Can you see them in your mind? Can you see the enormous ancient table—rich and dark—that smells like the forest? Can you see the tall, sturdy chairs lined with red velvet and beset with jewels? Can you see the goblets and platters piled high with delicious food? As I let Jesus take my hand (and I'm in a sparkling gown), I gather up my dress and take my seat.

What about you? What are you wearing? What are you feeling? What are you doing?

When we see ourselves this way—as seated at the table and called to complete the tasks God assigns us—we stop working so hard for acceptance. We stop caring about prestige. We no longer need to make a name for ourselves, because we're completely absorbed in Christ and the kingdom.

In this setting, we cease measuring ourselves against any other person. Why would we? We have our own seat, our own calling, and our own tasks. Plus, we're interdependent with one another, seated all together to make a holy dwelling place. Remember: we are included, which means we are chosen and seated together. The three verbs—included, chosen, and seated—are a triumvirate of power, a three-pronged strategy of verbs to understand who Jesus is and who we are in relation to Him.

We have a seat together at the table. We are chosen for this seat and included here. We are free to live our lives from a position of security, self-forgetfulness, and equality with others. We've already received the fullness of Christ and His righteousness. His power is available to accomplish all He calls us to do. Christ won a place for us, and we're seated in Him and with Him. We can stop fighting to win a spot.

I knew the Shadow Narrative all too well; people fighting for a seat at the table live in three toxic ways that I battled for most of my life. I believed I would be seated if I had what my Christian counselor called the three As: *appearance, affluence,* and *achievement.* My Shadow Narrative was all about how I believed if I were beautiful, I'd find a seat at the table. Or, if only we had more money, I'd have a seat at the table. And finally, and more important, I battled for a seat at the table through achievement. I thought that if only I could accomplish this one thing, then maybe I would finally have a seat at the table.

What is the table you eye as finally bringing you the life you've always wanted?

But then, I wondered what would happen if I truly believed I was already seated at the Greatest Table. What is this table like?

Now describe your seat in the heavenly realms with Jesus.

When my daughter suffered through her middle school lunchroom rejection, she sat by me while I was writing down my thoughts on Ephesians 2:6.

"Do you know what I'm writing about?" I ask her.

"What?" she says, sitting there on my lap before the computer screen.

"I'm writing about how Jesus tells us we have a seat at His table in the heavenly realms. We have our own special seat with Him." I quote Ephesians 2:6 to her.

She nods. My voice cracks, and I pray she can't tell I'm damming up a river of tears from my own memories of middle school popular tables and dances and parties; I store up vivid pictures of all the places I never sat.

"Do you know what that means?"

She rests her head on my shoulder, waiting.

"It means you have a seat at the table. It's strange to imagine it—it's in your mind, but it's real even though you can't see it—that you are a royal princess at the greatest table in the world. It's not in the physical realm, but you're *there*. I mean, you're here, but you're also there."

I'm floundering. I'm praying.

Nothing. No response.

"I want you to remember that when you go to the lunchroom. You are seated with Christ. Can you see it? Don't think about those popular girls. Don't think about them anymore. You have a seat at the best table already. You're wanted there. Jesus chose you for His table."

She turns her head up to the ceiling and closes her eyes. She's a little girl who needs to know she's seated at the table. She—and her mother, too—desperately need to believe it. I'm wiping away tears now. I better get it together before she slides off my lap and returns to her math homework and prime factorization.

"Yeah. I see it."

I can tell by the way she's smiling that she can. I see a sparkle in those eyes and a new hope rising up inside of her.

I'm no longer eleven years old, but when I enter a new place, I feel the same old insecurity. I wonder where I'm going to sit. I wonder where I belong. But now, I repeat, "I'm seated with Christ." It's not some moment of wishful thinking or some New Age mantra; it's a declaration of *who I am* in the heavenly realms.

I'm secure and called to perform the good works that God prepared in advance for me to do. I therefore have no concern about my place anymore. I know where I am. I know I belong.

When we greet each other, neither of us needs to feel either inferior or superior. We rejoice that we are seated at His table together. I feel honored and amazed at you as a beautiful creation who has a seat at the table with me.

If you know you have a seat at the Greatest Table with the Greatest King, take a few minutes to thank Him.

A NEW SEATED LIFE

Just as chosen people live in seven news ways in every circumstance and season of their lives (as treasured, belonging to a family, worshiping, conformed to Christ, displaying His splendor, completing the good works He prepared, and living according to a new pattern), seated people live differently.

• Seated people adore instead of obsess over appearance.

Instead of obsessing over their appearance, they *adore* Jesus and radiate His beauty. Instead of the pursuit of wealth and desire for affluence, seated people know they have *access* to all the riches of God's kingdom. Finally, seated people stop exhausting themselves with achievement; they simply *abide* with Christ and bear His fruit through their lives.

Seated people don't worry about their appearance because they are seated to adore Jesus. *The focus on appearance becomes a gaze in adoration.* Consider how in Psalm 34:5 we learn that "those who look to him are radiant; their faces are never covered with shame." Seated people radiate the beauty of Christ. They showcase His beauty through their bodies and faces.

I thought of my Shadow Narrative of endless diets, exercising to exhaustion, and layers of makeup to hide my imperfections. I thought of never feeling beautiful. But seated people? We radiate the beauty of Christ as we adore Him from our seats in the heavenly realms. King David wanted only to "gaze on the beauty of the Lord." He writes in Psalm 27:4,

> One thing I ask from the LORD,
>   this only do I seek:
> that I may dwell in the house of the LORD
>   all the days of my life,

to gaze on the beauty of the LORD
  and to seek him in his temple.

Imagine that Christ is radiating His beauty through your face and that now you move out into day, seeking to love people through your whole self. What do you think it means to "gaze on the beauty of the LORD"?

• **Seated people access God's riches instead of being consumed with affluence.**

My Shadow Narrative of fighting for a seat at the table of wealth meant that I always fantasized about earning more money. I resented our ministry paycheck that came from support from churches and individuals. I believed that I'd be happy and fulfilled if only we had more money. But then I considered how people seated at God's royal table live: They know they have access to all the riches of God's kingdom. Consider the following verses:

> Philippians 4:19: "My God will meet all your needs according to the riches of his glory in Christ Jesus."

> 2 Corinthians 9:8 "And God is able to bless you abundantly, so that in all things at all times, having all that you need, you will abound in every good work."

Circle all the "all" words. Think about what you need right now and when you need it. Write down what comes to mind.

All things

All times

All that you need

1 Timothy 6:17–19: "Command those who are rich in this present world not to be arrogant nor to put their hope in wealth, which is so uncertain, but to put their hope in God, who richly provides us with everything for our enjoyment. Command them to do good, to be rich in good deeds, and to be generous and willing to share. In this way they will lay up treasure for themselves as a firm foundation for the coming age, so that they may take hold of the life that is truly life."

Give an example of God "richly providing everything for your enjoyment."

What would a life look like that was "rich in good deeds"?

• Seated people abide with Christ to produce fruit instead of exhausting themselves with achievement.

People seated with Christ *abide* with Him. When Jesus says in John 15:4 to "remain" with Him, it means *abide, stay in place, be continually present* with Him. He promises in the next verse that "if you remain in me and I in you, you will bear much fruit; apart from me you can do nothing." How freeing it feels to know that I do not design or bring about the "fruit" or "good works" of my life! They are God-designed and Spirit-empowered. Our job is to abide and God produces fruit naturally through our lives.

But how do we "stay present" with Jesus? Think of the spiritual disciplines of prayer, Bible study, worship, confession, and any other practice that helps us connect to Jesus and build our relationship with Him.

Another way I think about abiding to bear fruit—instead of exhausting myself with achievement—is a statement a mentor gave me that has become a family motto. She said, "Be led and not driven." In other words, she encouraged me to think about my accomplishments as Spirit-inspired, Spirit-led, and Spirit-empowered (we'll discuss this in the coming weeks).

In Philippians 2:13, we read, "For it is God who works in you to will and to act in order to fulfill his good purpose." This verse means that God is working within us to give us the desire and the ability to accomplish those things He has designed for our lives. Additionally, Isaiah 26:12 says simply and beautifully, "Lord, you establish peace for us; all that we have accomplished you have done for us."

What makes you feel like you are "abiding" with Jesus? Do you have an example of a time you were abiding with Jesus and your life began to bear fruit naturally?

As I adored, accessed, and abided in my seat in the heavenly realms, I realized that everything I wanted in my life was already happening because I was with Jesus.

Years ago, I found a quote in a novel by Lorrie Moore as I browsed books in the public library. It's from the museum guide of the Hayden Planetarium. The guidebook states, "All seats provide equal viewing of the universe."[6] I read it out loud, and the truth of it seemed to catch in my throat. I emailed the media director at Hayden Planetarium to learn more about this quote. I corresponded with a woman who said that the planetarium is designed so that no matter where you sit, you see the exact same images. No matter where you sit, you won't miss any part of the show.

No matter where you sit, you won't miss anything. I almost burst into tears.

I imagine all the children on field trips racing into the planetarium auditorium as the doors swing open. I imagine them all fighting for the best seats in an arena that has no best seats. I imagine the calm voice of the tour guide saying, "Children, all seats provide equal viewing of the universe."

As I read about the planetarium, it seemed that some great voice of wisdom gently whispered in my ear. I realized that in every circumstance, I have full access to everything I need. I turned to my daughter and read it to her.

"Do you know what that means?" I asked. "It means that no matter where you are, you have an *equal chance* to perceive the beauty of God. All seats are equal. You can stop fighting for a special seat. Your seat *is* the special seat. *All* the seats are the special seats."

When I want to trade seats to find a better view, I'm going to sit tight and realize my equal chance to see—right where I am—the beautiful things God wants to show me. I'm seated in Christ, and it's a beautiful view. All seats provide equal love, equal access, equal blessing.

Two women I once envied invited me out to dinner. Sure enough, before I even took my first sip of coffee, one told of her plans for a lavish vacation including a chartered boat to a remote island. She talked about the gourmet dinners she'd enjoy with her well-dressed, popular children.

Guess how I responded?

I found myself *joyously laughing* with her about all the incredible experiences she would have with this amazing family God had given her. I talked about all the seafood and steaks she'd enjoy. I visualized us seated together in Christ in the heavenly realms. I knew that God had chosen to pour some wonderful things into my friend's life, and I felt—for the first time—freedom from jealousy or comparison.

When it was my turn to share about our glamorous plans for vacation, I talked about staying home, writing, walking in the woods, and baking. *All seats provide equal viewing of the universe.* My simple vacation could be just as filled with the glory of God as hers. But it went deeper than that; I didn't even want to compare. It seemed silly, like someone comparing avocados to coffee. Why would I? It makes no sense.

As I sat there at the restaurant and imagined myself seated with Christ, I didn't worry about feeling excluded, inferior, or superior. I'm seated with Christ at my special place in the heavenly realms. I'm included, chosen, and now *seated*. Therefore, I imagine my seat. I say in my mind, "I'm seated with Christ in the heavenly realms. I belong. I'm included. I'm totally secure. Now, how can I bless these people?"

Whenever I feel insecure in any setting, in fact, I think about blessing others. If I worry about teaching or mentoring or even cooking dinner, I imagine my seat and repeat in prayer, "I'm seated with Christ, and there are all sorts of good works God has prepared in advance for me to do. I'm available to do them, so Jesus please empower me right now to teach this lesson, mentor this woman, or cook this meal to bless others."

In large ways and small ways, I know I'm seated with Christ: When I'm vacuuming and cleaning toilets, I'm seated with Christ at a royal table. When I'm onstage giving a speech to a thousand people, I'm seated with Christ and no more important than when I'm cleaning the bathroom at home. When I'm raising my children, I'm seated with Christ. He chose these children for me to raise, and I'm the perfect mother for them. My children, too, are seated with Christ, and I can cease fretting about the lives God has planned for them.

Finally, when I feel frantic, like I'm not doing enough, or doing too much, I remember that I'm seated with Christ. Jesus ordered His day around the Father's *exact* instructions. No more, no less. Jesus says yes to what He's supposed to say yes to. He declines what He must decline. He travels here and there under divine order.

As you think about your special seat, and the tasks before you today, recall John 14:31 where Jesus says, "I love the Father and do exactly what my Father has commanded me." We can do exactly what God commands. Not what the culture says we must do, not what magazines or Pinterest tell us what to do, not what Christian bloggers tell us what we must do, but what the Father has commanded you and me to do.

When I look more closely at Jesus' life in the Gospel accounts, I note how He knows when to stop talking and when to speak. He knows when to get up and leave, and He knows when to stay. He does *exactly* what He's supposed to do. He doesn't consider what everyone else does. He does what He's supposed to do. He's following a different set of instructions.

Just a few verses earlier, we read that we can do exactly what Jesus instructs because the Holy Spirit teaches us "all things" and "reminds" us of everything we've been taught (John 14:26). If the Holy Spirit teaches us all things, can't we ask God for specific instructions for our day? We pray and ask, and then we order our day *exactly*.

Because you're seated in Christ at your own seat, this day will look nothing like your best friend's, your coworker's, or your neighbor's, or anyone else's pictures on social media.

What will it look like? It will look *exactly as it's supposed to look* because you're seated with Christ in the heavenly realms. You have your own calling today. You have your own "good works that God has prepared in advance" for you to do.

I don't need to worry about any other seat at this table in the heavenly realms. I just sit in my seat and understand that God is working in me to live the life He has planned for me.

As Theodore Roosevelt said, "Comparison is the thief of joy." I heard this quote years ago, but I didn't know how to stop comparing myself to others. Now I can. I can because I imagine, on a daily basis, that I'm seated with Christ in the heavenly realms.

Is there someone you've been comparing yourself to? Pause right now and thank God that you don't need to compare yourself with anyone else because you are seated with Christ in the heavenly realms.

WRITING YOUR SEATED STORY

The most wonderful part of writing *Seated with Christ* has been receiving letters from readers impacted by the book. One letter I received showcased such a strong Shadow Narrative and corresponding Savior Story that I asked for permission to feature it here. After you read it, I invite you to write your own story of "fighting for a seat" and then finally taking your seat with Jesus. Thanks to Paulina Foote for sharing her story below.

FEATURED SAVIOR STORY

I grew up in a lower middle-class family in Texas where my parents were missionaries. I did not get a very good high school education, and upon entering college I had to take a special reading class because my reading was so poor.

I have always felt like I did not have a seat anywhere. I have struggled with overeating and weight issues, and I have felt that because I didn't finish college and get a degree I was inferior. I grew up with enough but never enough. I always wanted to have a seat at the table with the rich and famous of our city. But now I have the knowledge of my seat at the Table with Jesus as the focus of my world.

At the table with Jesus I am wearing a beautiful long sweetheart neckline dress in gorgeous light pink with a big hoop taffeta skirt and rhinestones. No shoes, but perfectly pedicured feet. Jesus is wearing a tuxedo with a white tie, because, my darling, this is a white-tie event! The table is set with the most beautiful china and crystal and fresh flowers galore.

The smell in the air is most delightful and sweet and it makes me feel like I will stay here forever. I am weeping as I write this because, like you, I know for certain that I am seated with Christ. I'm sure if my husband of three years knew about the voice in my head that whispers "I'm seated" when we have arguments and disagreements, he would want to thank you too.

1. Name your Shadow Narratives.

In what areas of your life do you most compare yourself to others? Tell the story of how you compare (or have compared) yourself and the resulting jealousy.

Describe your longing for that "special seat" that you think will finally bring you life. What will that seat do for you and why?

2. Compose your Savior Story of being seated with Christ.

How is (or will) being seated with Christ changing how you think about your appearance?

How is (or will) being seated with Christ changing how you think about money?

What is (or will) being seated with Christ changing how you think about your achievements?

3. How do you as a seated person now live?

Compare the old you who was fighting for a seat at some table to the new, seated you.

4. Choose an image or object to remind you that you are seated with Christ.

Here you may want to write down the vivid description of your seat at the table with Jesus, or you might have another picture in your mind. Feel free to draw a picture here.

CONFESSION, REPENTANCE, AND RENEWAL

Confess to Jesus the ways you've been fighting for a seat apart from Him. List out your jealous thoughts. Also note any ways you have acted in superiority or inferiority. As you think about being included, chosen, and seated, ask God to help you interact with others based on this new identity. Ask God to help you repent, and invite Him to renew your mind to see how you are seated at the Greatest Table with the Greatest King. Talk to Jesus about your insecurities about your appearance, your concern over money or resources, and your fear of not accomplishing enough. Then reread Ephesians 2 aloud and thank God for the new you.

strengthened

Ephesians 3:14–21

"Look to the Lord and his strength; seek his face always."

—1 Chronicles 16:11

A MAGNIFICENT PRAYER FOR YOU

Read Ephesians 3:14–21.

Perhaps the most beautiful and powerful prayer in Scripture flows out of Paul's words in Ephesians 3:14–20. For context, as you read the first thirteen verses of Ephesians 3, you'll note that Paul continues his great theme of how included we are—chosen and seated together—and even describes the great mystery in Christ of our *togetherness in Him.*

Paul repeats this crucial word—*together*—three times: "This mystery is that through the gospel the Gentiles are heirs *together* with Israel, members *together* of one body, and sharers *together* in the promise in Christ Jesus" (v. 6). So far in this study you have three verbs to remember this supreme mystery: we are included in Christ, chosen by Christ, and seated with Christ.

The dominant image of having a seat at the table will help us cue all the data we need about this critical new reality. We are not alone; we deeply belong to one another in the most mysterious, profound, sublime partnership. We are an ensemble, an interdependent organism called "the body of Christ," and a holy dwelling place for Him. This together identity (included, chosen, seated) provides the solid foundation for what comes next in our understanding of Jesus and our new life in Him. Paul, after helping us recall our togetherness, reminds us that now "we may approach God with freedom and confidence." He shows us how to pray, especially in a moment of discouragement.

And his readers were indeed discouraged by Paul's situation. God's chosen servant, Paul, someone obviously called by God, loved by God, empowered by God, and protected by God was imprisoned, under house arrest in Rome. Why would God allow this suffering? How are we to think about God and His love for us in the midst of whatever "prison" we find ourselves in? Remember, Paul even writes in Ephesians 3:13, "I ask you, therefore, not to be discouraged because of my sufferings for you." Clearly, Paul recognized his suffering and did not ignore it. He claims in Colossians 1:24 the following: "I rejoice in what I am suffering." Before we read about Paul's response to his suffering, take a moment to consider the following questions:

What comes to mind when you think about a prison? How would a person normally feel if imprisoned and awaiting trial?

Think for another moment about your own "prisons" or suffering. What areas of your life make you feel tied down, deprived of rights, uncomfortable, or in suffering? These thoughts might become the beginning of your Shadow Narrative of suffering that Paul teaches us how to transform into the Savior Story.

Now let's consider the passage from Ephesians 3:

> For this reason I kneel before the Father, from whom every family in heaven and on earth derives its name. I pray that out of his glorious riches he may strengthen you with power through his Spirit in your inner being, so that Christ may dwell in your hearts through faith. And I pray that you, being rooted and established in love, may have power, together with all the Lord's holy people, to grasp how wide and long and high and deep is the love of Christ, and to know this love that surpasses knowledge—that you may be filled to the measure of all the fullness of God.

Now to him who is able to do immeasurably more than all we ask or imagine, according to his power that is at work within us, to him be glory in the church and in Christ Jesus throughout all generations, for ever and ever! Amen. (vv. 14–21)

I love this passage so much and find so much encouragement from it as I think about God's goodness and great love for us. In fact, this very passage sent me on a journey to ask how God was strengthening me in my inner being with what I called His "guarding" care.

In *Guarded by Christ: Knowing the God Who Rescues and Keeps Us*, I collected biblical evidence of how God operates in our inner being. This work helped strengthen me like never before, and I discovered a newfound maturity in Jesus. I focused, therefore, on the operative word "strengthened" because I knew I wasn't living strong in the Lord. I was too unsettled, immature, and weary. I desperately needed a Savior Story of strength.

We can ask several questions to understand God's work in our lives regarding this new verb "strengthened."

Where are we strengthened?

When are we strengthened?

How are we strengthened?

Why or for what purpose are we strengthened?

Who strengthens us?

What did God reveal to you in this passage? Did you discover, as I did, that we are strengthened in our inner being as we ask God to do so in prayer? I was amazed to think that this was something Paul prays for; it doesn't come automatically or without our intentional request.

I realized that we need strengthening "so that Christ may dwell in [our] hearts through faith" (v. 17). I struggled to understand this statement because, at first, it doesn't make sense. I had to ask: Why do we need strength to allow Christ to dwell in our hearts through faith? Is it because something daily battles this reality? Is it because our hearts—left to themselves—refuse to recognize the indwelling, all-powerful Christ within our souls?

It's as if Paul says, "You need strength to understand how Christ dwells within you. This isn't natural or within your human ability. This is something empowered by the Holy Spirit, so pray for it daily." We need strength to recognize the indwelling Christ that goes beyond our rational understanding. I'm beginning to realize that some things about the Christian faith exceed my understanding, and Paul acknowledges this too.

Twice Paul refers to experiences that go beyond or surpass the human mind's understanding. Paul highlights a knowledge of the love of Christ "that surpasses knowledge" and a God who does "immeasurably more than all we ask or imagine." Christ's power works within us in a way that goes beyond human understanding.

After years of considering what this power is for—and why it's so vital to understand how it operates in light of suffering, disappointment, and terrible external circum- stances—I realized that Paul urgently prays for the deepest kind of strengthening inside to endure suffering. When we consider how Paul composes these words from less than optimal conditions, we can see the whole point of our being strengthened: to know Christ's love and fullness and ability "to do immeasurably more than all we can ask or imagine, according to his power that is at work within us."

What in Paul's prayer encourages you?

DO NOT BE SURPRISED

Paul experienced all this love and fullness and power, yet God kept him under guard. Paul knew the "glorious riches" of God, but these riches did not release Paul from house arrest. This might not be the response we wanted, but Paul is talking about something better.

He points out something wonderful and magnificent about what it means to grow into true biblical maturity. He's talking about inner strength in Jesus that can withstand any suffering. He's talking about the kind of strength the woman in Proverbs 31 displays—the one who "is clothed with strength and dignity; she can laugh at the days to come." He's talking about the mature one described in James 1:4 who is "mature and complete, not lacking anything" and the one in Colossians 4:12 who "[stands] firm in all the will of God, mature and fully assured." He's finally talking about the mature people described in Psalm 112:7–8 who "have no fear of bad news; their hearts are steadfast, trusting in the LORD. Their hearts are secure, they will have no fear."

This I want. This kind of inner strength—this kind of biblical maturity—I desperately need. Otherwise, I'm constantly a victim to circumstances and that Shadow Narrative of inner fragility, instability, disordered thinking, and weakness. I turn away from difficult tasks because they unsettle me. I find instead that I hide away, missing out on all God has in store for me, because I'm afraid and weak and nervous like a bug or vampire hiding from the light. I seek comfort instead of character. I seek a change in circumstances instead of seeing my Savior in every situation.

But now, in light of Ephesians 3:14–21, I know that strengthened people live out of their inner being and the full privileges and resources of being a child of God. And they have a Savior Story of God's work in their lives through suffering.

Read Psalm 66:10–12, 16.

This morning, I thanked Jesus for testing and refining me. I thanked Him for the burdens that have imprisoned me. I thanked Him for our Savior Stories because "we went through fire and water, but you brought us to a place of abundance." And after understanding this wonderful story God is writing, the psalmist says in verse 16: "Come and hear, all you who fear God; let me tell you what he has done for me."

In this study, we are both listening and telling. We shaped our Savior Story of included, chosen, and seated, and now we have the opportunity to think of our stories of strength. When I ask, "How is God strengthening me?" it's not only a onetime kind of imparting of strength by the Holy Spirit. God uses something very special and strange in order to strengthen us in our inner being. He uses, among many things, *suffering*. I know this doesn't sound like something you wanted to read.

God will use our circumstances to strengthen us and draw us into intimacy with Him. Suffering trains us to depend on God as nothing else can. Billy Graham describes God's ultimate protection of our lives and claims, "God has not promised to shield us from trouble, but he has promised to protect us in the midst of trouble. Nothing can touch us apart from God's will. If something does touch us, we can be sure that it is for the purpose of building us up into a stronger and more effective witness so that God can use us . . ."[1] Graham helps us see how God is protecting us, and when difficulty comes into our lives, God is using it to *strengthen us to be of better service to Him.*

We can change our view of our problems in life when we believe God allows them and uses them. Graham famously said, "The will of God will not take us to where the grace of God cannot sustain us." God will sustain us wherever He brings us, and we have nothing to fear when suffering comes.

Our God is able to handle every problem in our lives. Walter Henrichsen, in *Disciples Are Made Not Born*, makes this challenging statement: "Every problem a person has is related to his concept of God. If you have a big God, you have small problems. If you have a small God, you have big problems. It is as simple as that. When your God is big, then every seeming problem becomes an opportunity. When your God is small, every problem becomes an obstacle."[2]

I'm someone who lived in the Shadow Narrative of a small God, where every problem in my life was a huge obstacle. Even my husband says I maximize every problem into a catastrophe instead of an opportunity. My own mother, a talented design seamstress, taught me that designers don't see problems but rather "special situations that are opportunities for embellishments." My mother doesn't like the word "problem" mentioned in her presence. She'll correct me to see the "special situation" and "opportunity for embellishment."

Still, I don't want adversity or suffering. Who does? I want instant strength and maturity. Scripture, however, teaches that God uses suffering to grow us. In fact, in 1 Peter 4:12–14, we're told "do not be surprised" at trials "as though something strange were happening" to you. James 1 tells us to consider our trials "pure joy" because "you know that the testing of your faith produces perseverance." He writes to encourage us to "let perseverance finish its work so that you may be mature and complete, not lacking anything." And finally, in 1 Peter 1:6–7, we're told about the refining fire of God where the trials and grief we suffer are proving our faith genuine and real.

I'm learning that stress and trials in life function as opportunities to trust and rely on God. They are invitations to enter God's presence. But perhaps most importantly, they are mechanisms for our growth and maturity. Without trial, we stay flimsy and immature inside.

Write down some of your current or past trials. How is God refining you and maturing you through this suffering?

A LESSON FROM A PROBLEM-FREE ENVIRONMENT

Consider the lesson from the trees in a research project called Biosphere 2. Biosphere 2 is a science research facility in Arizona built to be a "closed ecological system" to study growth of plants among other research projects. In this *problem-free environment,* something astonishing happened. The trees in Biosphere 2—enclosed and problem free—grew more rapidly than trees in the wild. But right before they were about to mature and bear incredible fruit, they toppled over, completely collapsing under their own weight.

What do you think went wrong? Why did these trees collapse without maturing? You'll never guess what scientists learned: the trees collapsed because of lack of stress from wind. The problem-free, enclosed system had no wind to stress the trees. Consider this:

> When plants and trees grow in the wild, the wind constantly keeps them moving. This causes a stress in the wooden load bearing structure of the tree. So, to compensate, the tree manages to grow something called the reaction wood (or stress wood). This stress wood usually has a different structure (in terms of cellulose or lignin content and more) and is able to position the tree where it'd get the best light, or other optimum resources. This is the reason why trees are able to contort towards best light and still survive loads in even awkward shapes.[3]

When I read that stress builds a special kind of strength in the tree that positions the "tree . . . [for] the best light," I thought of how my own stress positions me to God's light and His resources. I thought of bearing fruit and not collapsing under my own weight because God had built my inner being so strong. I remember this: Without stress, a tree can grow quickly, but it cannot support itself fully. It cannot withstand normal wear and tear and it will not survive. In other words, we, like the trees in Biosphere 2, need some stress in *order to thrive* in the long run.

In the midst of stress and trial and disappointment and anything that comes against our lives, I remember this from Paul's prayer in Ephesians 3:

Strengthened people live from their soul instead of external realities (v. 16).

Strengthened people live deeply connected to Jesus who dwells within them (v. 17).

Strengthened people grasp the unfathomable love of Christ (v.18).

Strengthened people live filled with the fullness of God (v. 19).

Strengthened people live from truth instead of their emotions (v. 19).

Strengthened people understand God's ability to do immeasurably more than they can ask or imagine (v. 20).

Reflect: Write down in your own words how a strengthened person responds to stress and suffering.

Now, contrast a strengthened person to one living a fragile, weak life. Think about the claim in Isaiah 40:29–31. Here we are told what God does for weak people.

> He gives strength to the weary
> and increases the power of the weak.
> Even youths grow tired and weary,
> and young men stumble and fall;
> but those who hope in the Lord
> will renew their strength.
> They will soar on wings like eagles;
> they will run and not grow weary,
> they will walk and not be faint.

Picture the weary, faint, fragile one. This person lives without an awareness of God within them, as though God's love were not operating. She lives as if something about Jesus is missing; she misses the "fullness of God." This person would also live as a victim of her moods, thoughts, and circumstances.

Finally, people like this have a dim view of God's ability to "do immeasurably more than they ask or imagine." They don't realize they are eagles soaring (and eagles rest on the thermal air currents to soar; they hardly use their own strength at all).[4] As a side note, when you think about the eagles and the lesson from the trees in Biosphere 2, you might be delighted to recall the quote by the Wright Brothers observing the birds in relation to man's first flight. They write, simply, "No bird soars in calm."[5]

I want to grow to the point where I can see my "problems" as helping me soar as the eagle and strengthening me like a mighty oak. I won't soar in problem-free calm.

What difficulties have helped you soar like the eagle? Are you facing something now that you can look at as an opportunity to become strengthened like an oak?

WEEK 4 | DAY 4

FULLNESS AND IMMEASURABLY MORE

I think about this person who forgets or doesn't realize God's strength within, and I see myself and that Shadow Narrative of weakness and weariness. I know because I battled anxiety, depression, and disordered thinking for nearly six years. I also tended toward narcissism or shame—both an excessive focus on self—and a hopeless feeling that nothing would ever change. How would God strengthen me in my inner being to know His love and to make me into the kind of woman I always wanted to be? Two packed phrases from this passage in Ephesians most unlocked God's strengthening within:

Fullness of God

Immeasurably more

What do you think is the fullness of God? What does this expression mean to you?

What picture comes to mind when you think of the phrase "immeasurably more"?

This past year, I wondered about the "fullness of God." Even though I realized I was included, chosen, and seated, I felt like I was missing some understanding about Jesus that kept me immature and imprisoned to my moods and circumstances.

As I explored the Bible and thought about Jesus' presence in my soul—that He was indeed dwelling within me—I made a list of all the characteristics of this God who guards our souls by His power. Jesus is

righteousness (Rom. 8:1; 2 Cor. 5:21)

peace (Isa. 9:6)

hope (Rom. 15:13)

power (Phil. 4:13)

our source of dying to self (Gal. 2:20)

And this list certainly doesn't exhaust everything that Jesus is. A year after writing *Guarded by Christ*, I knew what I had learned was a mere teaspoon of water compared to the ocean of who God is. I think of the fullness of God and His grace, mercy, and joy. Think of His

filling us with joy in His presence (Ps. 16:11)

unending help and provision in distress (Ps. 20)

kindness and compassion (Isa. 63:7)

wisdom (Dan. 2:20)

healing (Matt. 8–9)

masterful teaching (Mark 10:17–27)

authority (Matt. 28:18)

Oh, we could go on and on and on.

How would our ordinary days change if we believed we were "filled to the measure of all the fullness of God"?

For so many years, I didn't live out of the "fullness of God." I lived from *emptiness* and an *impoverished* mindset about all I was missing out on and everything I wanted but did not have. This Shadow Narrative of emptiness nearly stole my life. I was depressed, angry, and full of bitterness. I felt that old, poisonous ache that I wasn't living the life I was supposed to be living. I thought about the other neighborhoods my children could thrive in and the other cities I could be shopping in. I thought of the friends I didn't have, the thrift store wardrobe that was over ten years old, and the money we didn't have in the bank.

I cried about this empty life God had given me. Even with a wonderful husband and two daughters, life felt empty. This is a scheme of Satan. Remember, Eve was *in paradise*. She had it all, and Satan convinced her that *something was still missing*. The devil operates by tempting us to question our circumstances and doubt the fullness of God.

Have you ever felt this way? What parts of your life feel empty and impoverished?

Christians can tell a Savior Story of the "fullness of God" who does "immeasurably more than we ask or imagine." And He's a good God who wants to fill our lives with good things. But we forget the fullness and the immeasurably more. We live in a Shadow Narrative of emptiness.

One of my favorite Savior Stories of God's goodness and "immeasurably more" comes from a dear friend down the road. Her Savior Story is below. This friend had many needs in her life, and she was just beginning to trust in the goodness and provision of God. She always wondered if God really loved her and if she could trust Him with her needs. One day, she won a town prize—a Mother's Day Makeover—that she calls her "personal love letter" from God.

My dear friend Jenny Kelly writes this Savior Story of God's great love for her during a time in her life when she doubted if God loved her and saw her need.

FEATURED SAVIOR STORY

I know God loves me, but I forget.

When Heather asked me to write about the time God loved me so richly it was ridiculous, I had to ask her what she meant. I had completely forgotten the blessings from a Mother's Day Makeover. He'd woven it together like a personal love letter. How could I forget?

It's hard for me to trust God when prayers aren't answered today, this year, or this decade. But with every makeover prize it became clear that whenever I had wished, hoped, prayed, or begged, He heard me and was already preparing my future.

Heather and I sat together in church the Sunday our pastor dared us to ask God to amaze us with His love. I thought, "What a nice idea," and went on with my life as usual . . . until a few weeks later when I found out I won the Mother's Day Makeover and sat there actually amazed.

He provided what I needed when I hadn't thought to ask.

A few months before the contest my dentist explained I needed bridgework that would cost $12,000. While worrying over saving that amount up, the makeover happened and its sponsoring dentist provided the bridge at no cost. My own dentist is still a little sore about it!

At the time I'd recently lost quite a bit of weight and maintenance was intimidating. The makeover came with a free year gym membership, several outfits in my new size, and a photo shoot after the makeover I could use for motivation.

The makeover also provided a jewelry spree that happened to be from a jewelry company I was already obsessed with. Completely unnecessary, but it showed He was paying attention.

Heather can attest that my biggest struggle in life is my hatred for housecleaning. The makeover provided a company that cleaned my house while I was whisked away in a limousine to have my hair, nails, and makeup done. Unfortunately, they only did this once!

They threw my makeover reveal party at the same restaurant where my mom used to work and where my mom and my stepdad fell in love. They both came to the party and cheered me on.

And He brought me a lifelong dream. We bought my reveal dress in a store I'd wanted to shop in since I was a little girl. Once, back in my college days, I had decided that now that I was an adult I could walk in and see this out-of-my-league store I'd wondered about all my life. So I went right in and waltzed right up to a shimmering dress and located the tag. I turned it over, noticing it was printed on paper softer and thicker than a wedding invitation—and that was just the price tag. The price was so high I got scared and hurried out.

After forty years of dreaming and twenty years after I fled the store, this time I walked in and tried on several dresses. And they simply gifted me with my favorite. A complete reversal from my first visit. I could have gotten a dress in a different upscale boutique. But He arranged for me to win a dress from the store I'd always wanted to shop in.

The prizes covered almost everything I needed at that time in my life. Everything plus a Wii console. We already had one, so what was I going to do with another? Heather pursed her lips in a mischievous smile and told me her oldest daughter had just asked God for a Wii. The day after the makeover I brought it to their house. There are few joys greater than playing the role of God's delivery person.

It amazed me to see Him fulfill the long-forgotten dreams of the small girl I still feel like in my heart. Then and now these were things I wanted but would never buy for myself. God gave them to me for no good reason, with no earning, no scrimping, no saving, no fitting into a budget. Just "Here, these are for you."

An old little girl and a young little girl, asking God and receiving. I had a petulant urge to tell Heather's daughter how long I'd had to wait for my answered prayer dress. But she looked so happy with the Wii, I just couldn't do it.

She shouted and danced with excitement because God had heard her prayer.

What is your Shadow Narrative of emptiness? What do you always feel is missing?

Begin writing the Savior Story of your understanding the "fullness of Christ" in your life.

YOUR STRENGTHENING

Let's continue to examine that phrase that God "is able to do immeasurably more than all we ask or imagine" (v. 20). This was the Bible verse printed on our wedding program and the same verse framed above our family's kitchen table.

What I love about this phrase is that God far exceeds what we can ask or even dream about. Think about it: we go to Him with impossible prayer requests, and He can do *more*. We think about all our needs that we list out in our prayer journals, and He can do *more*.

I'm also amazed by the concept that God's work in our lives goes beyond what we can conceive. In 1 Corinthians 2:9, we read this: "However, as it is written: 'What no eye has seen, what no ear has heard, and what no human mind has conceived'—the things God has prepared for those who love him." We simply cannot predict or even dream up what God has in store for our lives—His good, pleasing, and perfect will (Rom. 12:2).

I'm old enough now to have collected beautiful stories of God's work on my behalf that far exceed my wildest dreams. I often tell the story, for example, of how I never wanted to move to Michigan for my PhD program because I'd never find my "Southern gentleman" there. I imagined a lonely, empty life. But I went out of obedience to God and with a surrendered heart. God not only brought me a Southern man, but one who had the epitome of a Southern name: Ashley (just like the famous character in *Gone with the Wind*). He didn't just bring me Ashley; God delivered two baby girls into my life, a new career, and a life I could never have predicted or even thought up in my imagination.

I also tell the story of how God made my publishing dreams come true in ways I couldn't have asked for or imagined. One of my favorite Savior Stories is about my writing career. I wrote a letter of surrender to Jesus one October because my dream of writing books just wasn't coming true. I was so discouraged, but I was indeed surrendered. I knew God loved me, but I couldn't have imagined what He was planning for me.

In my surrender letter to God, I let the dream die completely. I gave my little girl writing heart to God and agreed to write in all those smaller ways—blogging, lesson plans, letters—and I settled the issue in my heart that the book writing dream was *over*. I was at peace, seated with Christ in the heavenly realms, and ready for the other good works He had prepared for me that didn't include writing. It was a wonderful moment of knowing that *I didn't need writing* to prove myself, to feel important, to be somebody, or to be accepted. I could enjoy Jesus and the life He ordained for me, even if it didn't include my dream coming true. I thought my Savior Story was all about surrender and God helping me give up my dream.

What I didn't know is that my agent never gave up on my dream. I didn't know that he was still working, still submitting my manuscript, and still hoping for the perfect publisher for my book on being seated with Christ. And God still held my dream safely in His hands.

One cold winter night, I received a message that Moody Publishers in Chicago was interested in my book. Very interested. "What book? What are you talking about?" This was how dead the dream was. This was how long forgotten it was. I had to remind myself that there was this book on being seated with Christ that I had tried to publish but was never famous enough to have it noticed by name recognition.

An acquisitions editor would call me the next Tuesday. Moody Publishers would offer to buy my manuscript. They didn't care that I wasn't well known. They cared that I had written an honest and biblical book. And because everyone loved it so much and thought it was so powerful, they wanted to accelerate the process, secure the manuscript by April 15, and aim for an October release. God is funny. God's timing is perfect. God guards our dreams. He's not a trickster, a cruel God, or a distant one. He listens and knows.

I learned a whole new vocabulary: contracts, editors, design teams, publicity teams, fonts, callouts, first pages, final pages. Suddenly—and I mean suddenly—I found myself sitting in fancy Chicago restaurants and seeing my dream unfold in ways that were "immeasurably more than I could ask or imagine." I couldn't have dreamed of what God had in store for me in Chicago; I simply had no idea what God would do. It's been the life I've always wanted but didn't know it.

But God knew. He knows our hearts and knows exactly what we need. And He knew I felt stuck. It's as though something stuck in me became unstuck when I began publishing books.

And I was myself—the real me—living in the reality of being seated in Christ and not needing the book contract to make me somebody special. I knew I was already included, chosen, and seated, but now I was learning the "immeasurably more" of Jesus.

Along the way, some incredible things happened. One is that I never forgot the words from Joni Eareckson Tada that she'd rather be seated in her wheelchair knowing Jesus than be given the chance to walk without Him. When my amazing editor—who is now one of my dear friends—asked if there was one person in the world I might ask to write the foreword to my book, I said, "Joni Eareckson Tada." And guess what—she did. She wrote the most beautiful foreword for me. God can do anything. A few years later, I read letters from all over the world from readers of *Seated with Christ* and now *Guarded by Christ*. I recorded the audiobook, learned that *Seated* was being translated into Korean, and traveled across the nation to speak on overlooked verbs in Scripture. This is a life I didn't even know how to dream about. And even before all this, I had the fullness of Christ. But He does immeasurably more than we can ask or imagine.

Do you have a story of God doing more than you asked or could imagine?

1. Name your Shadow Narrative.

Part One: What story do you tell yourself over and over again in the following categories?

weariness

emptiness and something missing

2. Compose your Savior Story of strength, fullness, and immeasurably more. As you write, consider this quote from writer Hannah Whitall Smith:

> Could we but understand clearly the meaning of Paul's words "having nothing, yet possessing all things," all this would be at an end. For we would see that the one thing God wants of us is for us to empty ourselves of all our own things in order that we may depend on Him for everything, to discover that His purpose is to bring us to the place where we have nothing apart from Him.[6]

3. How do you as a strengthened person now live? Compare the old, weary and empty you to the strengthened you.

4. Choose an image or object to remind you that God strengthens you.
So far, I have God's hand for chosen, my seat at the table for seated, and perhaps an overflowing coffee mug for fullness. I also choose the eagle for the reminder of God's strength in my inner being. Recently, I think of mighty oak trees that grow strong because of wind.

CONFESSION, REPENTANCE, AND RENEWAL

As you pray to Jesus, confess to Him any areas of your life where you have failed to see His abundance and have chosen to live in emptiness instead. Ask Jesus to help you understand "how wide and long and high and deep" is His love. Thank Jesus for how you perceive His fullness and His provision that is "immeasurably more."

renewed

Ephesians 4:20–32

"With every morn my life afresh must break
The crust of self, gathered about me fresh;
That thy wind-spirit may rush in and shake
The darkness out of me, and rend the mesh
The spider-devils spin out of the flesh—
Eager to net the soul before it wake,
That it may slumberous lie, and listen to the snake."

—George MacDonald

CONFRONTING SIN WITH JESUS BY OUR SIDE

Read Ephesians 4 in its entirety, and underline all the characteristics of someone walking closely with God.

The next two weeks of our study will quite possibly challenge and transform you the most because, in these next chapters on being renewed and filled, we'll talk honestly about everything that holds us back from being the included, chosen, seated, and strengthened people we know we are.

Some theologians believe that the first three chapters of Ephesians "contain doctrine, the last three, exhortation,"[1] meaning that Ephesians 4 begins with instruction on *how to live*. It isn't always just an inaccurate view of God, a toxic mindset, or trials God allows that make us feel excluded, rejected, jealous, and weary. It's something else more terrible and distressing than you can imagine. It's what the Bible calls *sin*.

Sin, in simple terms, is going our own independent way from God; sin comprises the attitudes, actions, and words in our lives that don't please God. In James 4:7 we read, "If anyone, then, knows the good they ought to do and doesn't do it, it is sin for them" (v. 17).

Sin also represents the condition of our souls apart from God—the state of sin we inherited from the fall of Adam. Sin attempts to violate and corrupt everything God does and is doing.

What we must understand, however, is the biblical reality that having accepted Christ, we are *already* forgiven, already redeemed, already rescued, already made righteous before God because of Jesus. Jesus pays the penalty for our past, present, and *future* sin. The atonement is so far reaching that it extends, yes, even to the future.

God declares us righteous for all time before Him because of Christ who "has become . . . our righteousness" (1 Cor. 1:30). So why should we think about sin at all? Who cares? A mentor explained that Christians are saved from the *punishment* of sin but not always from the *consequence* of sin in our lives. Although our relationship with God is permanent, secure, and unchanging, our fellowship and intimacy with Jesus changes when we sin against God.

In order for us to experience once again that sweet fellowship with God, we confess our sin, agreeing with God about the areas of our sin, thank Him for His forgiveness, and walk again in the reality of that forgiveness. We need to *repent*, which means to turn in a new direction away from sin. Finally, we also ask God for wisdom if we need to restore anything, reconcile any relationship, or repair any damage our sin has caused.

Failing to confess sin—walking in any area of rebellion or independence from God—is to "give the devil a foothold" (Eph. 4:27) to work distress and destruction. It grieves the Holy Spirit (Eph. 4:30), blocks His power in our life (1 Thess. 5:19), and creates a barrier that prevents us from experiencing intimacy with God.

Psalm 66:18 explains that "if I had cherished sin in my heart, the Lord would not have listened." I've learned that when I feel distant from God, I ask the Holy Spirit to point out any area of my life that doesn't please Him. If I'm experiencing increasing "trouble and distress" (Rom. 2:9), I ask God to shine His spotlight on any place I have given the devil a foothold.

No matter how many years a person has been a Christian—and no matter how mature she believes herself to be—she can never escape the need for regular confession and repentance. These practices constitute a healthy diet of the Christian soul because we often forget the dangers and consequences of sin working within us.

Is confession a regular part of your Christian life? Why is it important to be aware of the need for confession and repentance, even for a mature Christian? What can happen to our walk with Christ when these disciplines are neglected?

As you read Ephesians 4, you might have felt discouraged and even condemned. Instead of condemnation, the Holy Spirit works to point out areas of specific sin and lead you immediately to the joy of forgiveness. Roy and Revel Hession, in *We Would See Jesus*, explain this:

> Whenever a sense of sin lies upon on conscience, two persons, it seems, fight to get hold of that conviction—the devil and the Holy Spirit. The devil wants to get hold of it in order to take it and us to Sinai, and there condemn us and bring us into bondage. The Holy Spirit, however wants take us and our sin to Calvary, there to bring us through the door to peace and freedom.[2]

The Holy Spirit always convicts us with the accompanying hope of peace and freedom of forgiveness, while Satan keeps us accused, condemned, and striving under what the Hessions call "bondage."

When I read Ephesians 4, then, I ask God about the areas of my life—especially marriage and motherhood—where I need to confess a lack of humility and gentleness. I ask God to show me where I haven't built unity. I let the Holy Spirit reveal any areas of greed, impurity, deceit, anger, and unwholesome talk. I don't want to grieve the Holy Spirit with gossip, bitterness, an unforgiving heart, or any unkindness. After thinking through Ephesians 4, I feel like a failure, but then I immediately apply Romans 8:1 and how "there is now no condemnation for those who are in Christ Jesus." I'm not condemned, now or ever, so I can confess my sin, repent, and immediately restore intimacy with Jesus. When I'm confessing sin and walking afresh in obedience to God, I invite a fresh empowerment of the Holy Spirit (the subject of next week's study).

We learn to hold two things in tension: the attention to the problem of sin within and the reality that in Christ we're declared righteous and perfect before God. First John 1:8–10 says:

> If we claim to be without sin, we deceive ourselves and the truth is not in us. If we confess our sins, he is faithful and just and will forgive us our sins and purify us from all unrighteousness. If we claim we have not sinned, we make him out to be a liar and his word is not in us.

Note Paul's understanding in Romans 7:17 about the "sin living in [him]" separate from his redeemed soul.

This morning, I read a sermon by Charles Spurgeon, delivered in 1856, that helped me understand the power of sin within me even as a believer declared righteous before God. Spurgeon writes,

> When a man is saved by divine grace, he is *not wholly cleansed from the corruption of his heart*. When we believe in Jesus Christ all our sins are pardoned; yet the power of sin, albeit that it is weakened and kept under by the dominion of the new-born nature which God doth infuse into our souls, doth not cease. . . .

> I hold that there is in every Christian two natures, as distinct as were the two natures of the God-Man Christ Jesus. There is one nature which cannot sin, because it is born of God—a spiritual nature, coming directly from heaven, as pure and as perfect as God himself, who is the author of it; and there is also in man that ancient nature which, by the fall of Adam, hath become altogether vile, corrupt, sinful, and devilish.

There remains in the heart of the Christian a nature which cannot do that which is right, any more than it could before regeneration, and which is as evil as it was before the new birth—as sinful, as altogether hostile to God's laws, as ever it was.[3]

Spurgeon's sermon explains that one nature within us cannot sin—that part of us stays guarded by Christ's righteousness at all times—but there's another part of us that "cannot do what is right" and stays "hostile to God's laws." This I feel. This I know. I understand what Paul says in Romans 7:

> For I know that good itself does not dwell in me, that is, in my sinful nature. For I have the desire to do what is good, but I cannot carry it out. For I do not do the good I want to do, but the evil I do not want to do—this I keep on doing. Now if I do what I do not want to do, it is no longer I who do it, but it is sin living in me that does it.
>
> So I find this law at work: Although I want to do good, evil is right there with me. For in my inner being I delight in God's law; but I see another law at work in me, waging war against the law of my mind and making me a prisoner of the law of sin at work within me. What a wretched man I am! Who will rescue me from this body that is subject to death? Thanks be to God, who delivers me through Jesus Christ our Lord! (vv. 18–25)

Have you experienced what Paul discusses in Romans 7? Write down some examples when you have not been able to do what you want to do and instead do what you don't want to do.

INNER TRAITOR

Reading Ephesians 4 attunes us to the ways we fall short of godliness and how our "old self" corrupts us with deceitful desires. Spurgeon prompts us to consider how this old sin nature always works within us to restrain and thwart the goodness of God in our lives. He discusses the terrible danger we are under because of sin all the time, and he so beautifully states:

> A Christian is a perpetual miracle. Every hour that I am preserved from sinning is an hour of as divine a might as that which saw a now-born world swathed in its darkness and heard "the morning stars sing for joy." Did ye never think how great is the danger to which a Christian is exposed from his indwelling sin? . . . Christian! Mind thy danger! There is not a man in battle so much in danger from the shot, as thou art from thine own sin. Thou carriest in thy soul an infamous traitor.[4]

When I read Spurgeon, I feel swept up in the power of divine mercy, of God's infinite grace, that performs a miracle in my nature every single day to keep me free from the power of sin that wants to kill, steal, and destroy my life. Although within me I carry an "infamous traitor," I have the indwelling Christ proclaiming my righteousness and applying the remedy for sin, the way out of temptation, and His strength to "keep in step with the Spirit" (Gal. 5:25). When I wrote *Guarded by Christ*, I desperately needed to apply Christ's righteousness to my feelings of condemnation and shame, but I also now need to understand the reality of sin working within me still.

As I began to walk with Jesus and make godly choices as a college student, my older sister used the expression "flirting with sin" when she thought I was beginning to make poor choices. She would say, "Heather, you need to stop doing that. It's flirting with sin." She meant that, although I wasn't necessarily doing anything against the law or violating a commandment in Scripture, I would often position myself to fall into temptation. Either I dated men who didn't share my love of Jesus or I would attend parties and choose activities that only led me away from Jesus, not toward Him.

Scripture talks about "sowing to please the flesh" instead of the spirit. Galatians 6:8 makes the sobering promise that "whoever sows to please their flesh, from the flesh will reap destruction; whoever sows to please the Spirit, from the Spirit will reap eternal life." So much of my life was sowing to please the flesh and not the Spirit as I walked near fire all the time and hoped I wouldn't get burned.

Spurgeon says "You have corruption in your heart: watch for the first spark, lest it set your soul on fire."[5] My Christian friends at the time also said to avoid the "near occasion of sin" and walk as far away from temptation as I could. I learned that sin "so easily entangles" (Heb. 12:1). I learned I had an enemy of my soul that wants me entangled, hindered, and ultimately in bondage to sin.

I knew I often sinned against God. It was a terrible feeling to come under the conviction of the Holy Spirit. I hated that feeling of guilt and sorrow, but over time, the conviction of the Holy Spirit became a beautiful and joyful mechanism for growth. I could ask Jesus, "Is there anything in my life that doesn't please You?" because I knew that confession and repentance invited a wonderful, precious renewal of God's work in my life. We don't need to fear God's pointing out of sin in our life. A mentor said, "I *love* being convicted of sin. I *want* to be convicted of sin. I like it because then I grow closer to Jesus as I rid my life of sin."

By following God in surrender and obedience, we allow God's spirit to flow unhindered, or, in the words of Eugene Peterson, "we get out of the way of what God is doing."[6] In Galatians 5:16–18, Paul explains that we have a choice to walk "by the Spirit" instead of the flesh (the old, sin nature) because our two natures still exist in conflict with each other until we reach heaven. We know we aren't in step with the Spirit because, according to Paul in verses 19–23, "the acts of the flesh are obvious: sexual immorality, impurity and debauchery; idolatry and witchcraft; hatred, discord, jealousy, fits of rage, selfish ambition, dissensions, factions and envy; drunkenness, orgies, and the like."

He contrasts this sinful nature with "the fruit of the Spirit . . . love, joy, peace, forbearance, kindness, goodness, faithfulness, gentleness and self-control." Paul calls us to "keep in step with the Spirit" to live according to the "new self" from our Ephesians 4 passage. The Holy Spirit brings peace and joy and freedom to your soul, but sin enslaves you and seeks to destroy your life.

Consider the following list to understand more about sin:

- Sin desires to rule over you (Gen. 4:7; Rom. 6:17)
- Sin hinders your relationship with God (Isa. 59:2)
- Sin brings trouble and distress into your life (Rom. 2:9)
- Sin is still living in, or operative within a believer (Rom. 7:17–20)
- Sin is anything that doesn't spring from faith in God (Rom. 14:23)
- Sin contaminates our body and spirit (2 Cor. 7:1)
- Sin entangles us and keeps us from the life God has for us (Heb. 12:1)
- Sin is often obvious and easy to see (Gal. 5:19–21)
- Sin can make us feel sapped of strength, like a heavy hand is upon us, and that we're groaning inside (Ps. 32:3–5)
- Sin is a real struggle (Heb.12:4)
- Sin is our death sentence apart from Jesus (Rom. 6:23)
- Sin begins with desire and will ultimately lead to death (James 1:15)
- Sin affects everyone, and we all need to have a habit of confession (1 John 1:5–10)

Has anything on this list surprised you?

What is wonderful about Ephesians 4 is the invitation to put off the old, sinful self and "be renewed in the spirit of your mind" (v. 23 NASB). Reread Ephesians 4 in its entirety and make a list of areas of sin you see.

Scripture is often very clear about the kinds of behaviors and attitudes that do not please God. I could spend the whole evening confessing to God all the ways I did not speak in ways that were "helpful for building others up according to their needs, that it may benefit those who listen" (v. 29). Was my speech helpful and encouraging? Did it always benefit those who listened?

As I write down my sins to confess in my journal, I immediately write in gigantic letters 1 John 1:9 (sometimes in bright red ink to remember the blood of Christ). I'm forgiven and cleansed as I confess. I repent by telling God I desire to move in the opposite direction of this sin, and I know I have a clean heart before Him.

I sometimes recite Psalm 51, King David's confession after Nathan the prophet confronted him when he committed adultery with Bathsheba and then had her innocent husband killed. This is a powerful and beautiful psalm to consider as you struggle with lingering guilt or shame over any sexual sin in particular. You are not alone, and you are not the first person to sin greatly against the God you love. David writes:

> Have mercy on me, O God,
>   according to your unfailing love;
> according to your great compassion
>   blot out my transgressions.
> Wash away all my iniquity
>   and cleanse me from my sin.
>
> For I know my transgressions,
>   and my sin is always before me.
> Against you, you only, have I sinned
>   and done what is evil in your sight. . . .

Cleanse me with hyssop, and I will be clean;
  wash me, and I will be whiter than snow.
Let me hear joy and gladness;
  let the bones you have crushed rejoice.
Hide your face from my sins
  and blot out all my iniquity.

Create in me a pure heart, O God,
  and renew a steadfast spirit within me.
Do not cast me from your presence
  or take your Holy Spirit from me.
Restore to me the joy of your salvation
  and grant me a willing spirit, to sustain me.

Then I will teach transgressors your ways,
  so that sinners will turn back to you.
Deliver me from the guilt of bloodshed, O God,
  you who are God my Savior,
  and my tongue will sing of your righteousness.
Open my lips, Lord,
  and my mouth will declare your praise.
You do not delight in sacrifice, or I would bring it;
  you do not take pleasure in burnt offerings.
My sacrifice, O God, is a broken spirit;
  a broken and contrite heart
  you, God, will not despise.

I love how David describes the forgiveness of God as a washing, cleansing, and a blotting out.

What did you notice about the way David describes sin? How does David describe forgiveness? After David experiences the cleansing of God, what happens next?

Begin a soul inventory of areas of your life that give the devil a foothold, that are "flirting with sin" or obvious areas of disobedience. As you write, continue to quote Romans 8:1 and how you are not condemned, now or ever. Also write down and memorize 1 John 1:9: "If we confess our sins, he is faithful and just and will forgive us our sins and purify us from all unrighteousness."

WEEK 5 | DAY 3

A NEW MINDSET

Let's look at our next passage in Ephesians 4 to understand more about sin and how to live "in step with the Spirit."

> That however, is not the way of life you learned when you heard about Christ and were taught in him in accordance with the truth that is in Jesus. You were taught, with regard to your former way of life, to put off your old self, which is being corrupted by its deceitful desires; to be made new in the attitude of your minds; and to put on the new self, created to be like God in true righteousness and holiness. (vv. 20–24)

That expression "be made new" is, in the Greek, "renewed."

I just love the verb *renew*. I think of fresh, vibrant, sweet-smelling things like when the forest is new again in springtime. I think of new life and strength and all the other related verbs like revitalize, reenergize, regenerate, revive, reinvigorate, and restore.

Think of pruning dead things to create room for the new. Think of a complete overhaul of your old, worn-out self. David talks about his own renewal like this: "You turned my wailing into dancing; you removed my sackcloth and clothed me with joy" (Ps. 30:11). What comes to your mind when you hear the expressions "be made new" or "renewed"?

Christians aren't just included, chosen, seated, and strengthened; we live as *daily renewed*. In Colossians 3:9–10, we learn that you have "taken off your old self with its practices and have put on the new self, which is being renewed in knowledge in the image of its Creator." Both Colossians and Ephesians, then, talk about putting on the "new self." But what is this new you? Can we apply our set of questions to the verb "renew"?

Who makes us new?

When are we renewed?

How are we made new?

Where is this renewal happening?

What's different about renewed people?

Why is He making us new?

Before we delve into the passage, let's remember: God specializes in *renewal*. Consider the following Bible verses and take a few notes based on the question below each one:

• 2 Corinthians 5:17: "Therefore, if anyone is in Christ, the new creation has come: The old has gone, the new is here!"

What comes to mind when you think of yourself as a "new creation"? What images flow through your mind?

- 1 Samuel 10:6: "The Spirit of the LORD will come powerfully upon you, and you will prophesy with them; and you will be changed into a different person."

When you think about being "changed into a different person," what parts of you would you want God to dramatically change?

- Romans 6:4: "We were therefore buried with him through baptism into death in order that, just as Christ was raised from the dead through the glory of the Father, we too may live a new life."

Write down anything that comes to mind when you think about living a "new life."

- Ephesians 4:22–24: "You were taught to be made new in the attitude of your minds; and to put on the new self, created to be like God in true righteousness and holiness."

Why do you think this passage says to be made new in the "attitude of your mind" and not "in the action of your life"?

- Psalm 40:3: "He put a new song in my mouth, a hymn of praise to our God. Many will see and fear the LORD and put their trust in him."

If you composed a song to God about all He has done for you and how wonderful He is, what would some of the lyrics be?

- Isaiah 43:19: "See, I am doing a new thing! Now it springs up; do you not perceive it? I am making a way in the wilderness and streams in the wasteland."

Write down the biggest problem you have in your life right now. Tell God that you trust Him that He is doing a new thing and making a way for you.

- Ezekiel 11:19: "I will give them an undivided heart and put a new spirit in them; I will remove from them their heart of stone and give them a heart of flesh."

What do you think an "undivided heart" is like?

- Isaiah 62:2: ". . . you will be called by a new name that the mouth of the LORD will bestow."

If you had to pick your new name based on some fruit of the Spirit, what would it be?

I love this last question because of a conversation I recently enjoyed with my sister. Twice in her life, someone told her, "You remind me of hope." Her life embodied a spiritual principle that people noticed. She even received a gift of the word HOPE framed for her wall from one of those friends.

When people look at your life, what word would come to mind? As I grow into increasing maturity, I pray that one day, my life might remind others of joy and peace or perhaps kindness. Too often, I fear I remind people of struggle or stress or self-promotion. Could our lives ever serve as living representations of what God had worked most deeply into us? Oh, Jesus has so much to change in me first!

I'm sitting in my chair by the weeping cherry tree, sipping my routine hazelnut coffee, reading the Bible and thinking about the past and all the ways I need to mature and grow when, like lightning in my soul, I remember *God changes names.* He takes the old you and gives you a new identity, one not rooted in all the past limitations or Shadow Narratives, but *a totally new you.*

He often takes someone and turns their identity into the opposite of what they once were (or who others believed they were). Abram (who had no children yet) now becomes Abraham (the father of many). Sarai (who also had no children yet) becomes Sarah (a princess and mother of nations). You can read about this in Genesis 17.

But it gets better as you keep reading the Bible. Jacob becomes *Israel*, Simon becomes *Peter*, Saul becomes *Paul*. All now manifest the power of God in stunning, overwhelming ways. I wonder if the new name helped them remember. I wonder if they slipped back into using their old names and had to say, "Oh, I'm sorry! That's not actually me anymore. I have a new name I go by now. And by the way, this new name means *I'm this awesome new person and chosen by God to do amazing things! I'm included, chosen, seated, strengthened, and now renewed! So remember the new me.*"

I tell my friend that I don't want to live in the *past me* anymore; I want to live in the new identity God gives me. God will one day actually assign me a new name (see Rev. 2:17), but right now, as a child of God, I am "crucified with Christ and I no longer live, but Christ lives in me" (Gal. 2:20). I have *His* name, really.

He changes our name. We are new people. We become the opposite of that identity that most drags us down. I like to think the new me has something to do with hope instead of despair, peace instead of anxiety, abundance instead of emptiness, and connection instead of loneliness.

Consider the part of your personality that most drags you down, harms you, or causes you to sin against God. Write down that one word and draw an arrow across the page. Then give yourself a new name. I wrote down my own top three to start our list.

THE OLD PART OF YOU	THE NEW NAME FOR THIS AREA OF YOUR LIFE
I was Despair ⟶	I am now Joy
I was Anxiety ⟶	I am now Peace
I was Self-Obsessed ⟶	I am now Savior-Focused

I'm so glad God changes names. He determines who I am, not my past. He teaches me how to put on my new self each day. He's renewing my whole life right now.

And He's doing this for you too!

WEEK 5 | DAY 4

OLD SELF AND NEW SELF

Consider again this passage:

> You were taught, with regard to your former way of life, to put off your old self, which is being corrupted by its deceitful desires; to be made new in the attitude of your minds; and to put on the new self, created to be like God in true righteousness and holiness. (Ephesians 4:22–24)

Did you notice in yesterday's question something interesting about your answers? I noticed that, unlike our other verbs, "renew" *depends on our cooperation.* We put off our old self. We put on our new self. We somehow participate in this renewal by the power of the Holy Spirit.

Now, let's discuss the old self that we put off.

Underline the phrases *former way of life* and *old self.*

Circle the word *corrupted.*

Circle the words *deceitful desires.*

When I first went into therapy for anxiety and depression in my late twenties, the Christian counselor—one of the wisest and most skilled I have ever met—invited me to consider the "false self" and the "real self" based on the old and new self from the Bible. He instructed me to consider what my personal "old self" looks like—that false, former way of life apart from Jesus. He even suggested bringing my husband—or anyone who knows me best—to help me with this task of identifying the works of my flesh in my life. This way, I would know when I was out of step with God's spirit or living according to former sinful patterns. I loved this activity because I discovered some unusual but highly revealing traits of my "old self" and "flesh."

When I'm out of step with God's Spirit, seven things happen right away to me personally: I become a gossiper and complainer; I believe I'm fat and ugly; I become obsessed with wanting a new, bigger, and lavishly decorated house; I desire more and more wealth and prestige; I begin to detest motherhood and marriage; I don't care about anyone's needs but my own; and I want comfort and pleasure above all else.

When I'm in step with God's Spirit, however, I know it so quickly:

- Instead of a gossiper and complainer, I'm an encourager and rejoicing.
- Instead of focusing on my appearance, I adore Jesus and radiate His love.
- Instead of wanting more, I'm content with what I have.
- Instead of greed, I want to give more and more of my resources away.
- Instead of detesting my God-given roles, I embrace them with delight and fresh energy.
- Instead of self-focus, I become concerned and compassionate about others and want to tell them about Jesus.
- Instead of comfort and pleasure, I feel strengthened to be uncomfortable and inconvenienced.

Oh, the flesh! Sometimes it's so discouraging to think about all the ways we live according to our old self. Because I'm in my forties, my particular sin patterns— while just as poisonous—aren't as dramatic on the surface as when I was younger. I lived in so much darkness that it's hard to describe. Look at those words *corrupted* and *deceitful desires* and imagine all the corrupt and deceitful traps including sexual impurity, drunkenness, lying, foul language, dishonoring parents, lust, greed, and gluttony. The list continues.

If you are reading this, you might feel the burn of shame rising in your face. Let me tell you this: nobody is shocked by your sin. I've been in ministry for nearly twenty-five years, and I can tell you that each girl who comes to me with her secret, private, horrifying sin thinks she's the only one on earth who ever thought those things or did those things. Not true!

Not only are you not alone in your sin, but think about this: Paul was the "worst of sinners"; he approved the murder of Christians. You might think you are the "worst of sinners," but Jesus wants to flood His light to conquer all the darkness inside of you as you come to Him. You are seated together at the table, and He sits beside you, ready and waiting to cleanse you. God will forgive, cleanse, and renew you.

And He can do it right now.

* * * *

I'm in sweatpants and an old Penn State T-shirt in my cluttered home office to finish the talk that I'm preparing for college women. I'm asking God to show me what to say to these women who have so much regret in their heart over sexual sin, bad choices, and all the ways they've hurt and disappointed people. They desire to change, but they don't know where to begin. They just feel guilty and ashamed all day long.

I hear a knock at my door. A woman from church I barely know stands on the front step. She's here for me to sign books for Christmas presents. I invite her upstairs to my office, and I awkwardly suggest that she might sit in the little blue toddler chair by my desk that's left over from a decade ago when my now-teens were little girls.

We begin talking about what Jesus is doing in our hearts—me in my sweats and she in the absurdly small blue chair, her knees practically up to her chin and I tell her that I'm writing this talk for the college women. Then I ask, "If you could tell the young women anything about sin and changing their lives, what would you say?"

She says, "Tell them about my weather app."

Then she proceeds to describe how the weather app on her phone announced that very morning that, in winter, *the sun is the exact same distance from the earth as it is in summer. The only difference is the tilt.*

"The tilt!" she says. "Just a slight tilt makes all the difference from darkness to light, from bitter winter to the warmth of summer! The women just need to tilt back to Jesus. He has not changed His distance from them. He is as near as He ever was and always will be."

In other words, Jesus is always near you in the exact same way—He never moves away from you. *The only difference is a slight tilt of your heart and life from the shadows and into the light.* If you looked at a simulation of the earth orbiting the sun, you would observe how it tilts into shadow as it rotates, and this causes either the beautiful warmth and renewal of summer or the bitter and empty landscape of winter. But the sun—like the Son—has never changed its location. The slightest tilt back toward the sun changes everything.

Many of us live in darkness and shadow. Maybe we're hiding because of secret desire—some hidden thing related to sexual sin, pornography, addiction, or ways we treat our own bodies. Our Shadow Narrative is this hidden darkness inside of us. Maybe we feel like our past—things done to us and things we've done to others—is our personal darkness.

Maybe our darkness is our mental health. Our darkness might be ways we've broken the law or how we've cheated or lied. We feel like it's bitter cold in our heart because of any number of things—disappointments, anger toward our parents, jealousy about other girls, and of course, all the sin we can't get rid of. The prophet Isaiah said it best in Isaiah 59:9: "We look for light, but all is darkness; for brightness, but we walk in deep shadows."

When you tilt back toward Jesus through bringing your sin into the light in His presence, it's the smallest little shift in your heart that brings you out of darkness. Jesus declares, in John 8:12, "I am the light of the world. Whoever follows me will never walk in darkness, but will have the light of life," just as David proclaimed, "God turns my darkness into light" (Ps. 18:28). And, in this light, according to 1 John 1:7, you "have fellowship with one another."

There's something about tilting back toward Jesus that allows the light of His presence and His truth to shine into the darkest places of our hearts. There's something about Jesus that invites people to come out of the shadows and live in this wonderful light where you find Jesus and the hope, beauty, peace, joy, and belonging He offers you in the family of God.

In order to "put on the new self" and walk in the light of renewal, we first take off the old self through confession of sin and repentance. Allow the Holy Spirit to shine light into areas of darkness in your heart and point out the sin you need to confess. This is the Holy Spirit's job in your life and nobody else's. In John 16:7–15, we learn that the Holy Spirit is the one who will point out sin and "guide you into all truth."

Let's pause right here. If the Holy Spirit has brought something to your mind, confess it and rest quietly before the Lord for a few minutes, thanking Him for shining light in an area of darkness.

My own Savior Story of being "renewed" spans a lifetime of confession and re-pentance, beginning with dating relationships and partying as a college student all the way till this very moment when I ask God if there is anything in my life that doesn't please Him. God is so faithful to help me cast off what entangles me—whether a bad attitude, selfish ambition, and bitterness (among so many other sins)—and guide me into new paths of righteousness. My Savior Story on renewal always begins with God cleansing me and helping me daily put on the "new self." Putting on the new self, in the Greek translation, means to "slip into like cloth-ing," so it makes perfect sense when Paul later writes to "clothe yourselves with compassion, kindness, humility, gentleness and patience" (Col. 3:12).

While slipping into clothing sounds easy, remember that Paul continues by advising "put to death, therefore, whatever belongs to your earthly nature: sexual immorality, impurity, lust, evil desires, and greed, which is idolatry." As we read verses like this one, I encourage us to pray that God points out sin specifically, that He gives us the desire and the power to confess our sins and obey Him in these areas.

What parts of your earthly nature can you start putting to death right now?

What does Paul tell us to put on? What does the new you with these traits look like?

The good girl. That's what I was always known as. I have always encouraged others to do the right thing and I set the bar high for myself. So how did I find myself sitting in a counselor's office sobbing because he had just told me it was time to decide who I really was? Was I a Christ follower who recognized my sin and wanted to move toward repentance? Or was I going to stay in the extramarital relationship that had rooted itself into my life and risk my marriage, reputation, and the unity of our church?

There were moments when I thought the damage would have been worth not having to go back to feeling trapped in a marriage that had left me broken, hurting, and empty. But there was something about the Holy Spirit's steady whisper that gave me a sense of hope that it was going to be okay. It was later in that same room, as I repented of my sin, a wall was torn down and I found myself in the arms of my husband who would not let me go, and through his own tears reassured me, "I know you, and if I had not neglected you, you never would have made this choice."

Contrary to his words, it was my choice, and I am the only one responsible for it, but I am so thankful for the work that God started in both of us that day. Now, years later, as I look back, it takes my breath away to see that what was meant for evil was used for good, and our marriage is stronger than ever and growing stronger still. Proverbs 28:13 says, "Whoever conceals their sins does not prosper, but the one who confesses and renounces them finds mercy." I am so grateful that God's Word does not return void.

FOR YOUR LIFETIME

As you look back over your life, I hope you've seen how Jesus has renewed you day by day. Remember that His renewal never ends. In the book of Ruth, an elderly mother-in-law, Naomi, who most would say grew old and beyond hope, sees God's unexpected renewal through her daughter-in-law.

In a beautiful moment when Naomi learns she is a grandmother, the women gather around her and proclaim thanksgiving and praise over the "guardian-redeemer" who is both Boaz (who married Ruth) and a picture of our future Redeemer, Jesus Christ. The women cry, "Praise be to the LORD, who this day has not left you without a guardian-redeemer. May he become famous throughout Israel! He will renew your life and sustain you in your old age" (Ruth 4:14–15).

I love that promise of renewal in old age. Another passage speaks to renewal in a way that brings hope to my soul. In Psalm 92, we read this in verses 12–15:

> The righteous will flourish like a palm tree,
>   they will grow like a cedar of Lebanon;
>   planted in the house of the LORD,
>   they will flourish in the courts of our God.
> They will still bear fruit in old age,
>   they will stay fresh and green,
>   proclaiming, "The LORD is upright;
>   he is my Rock, and there is no wickedness in him."

Our God renews us so we flourish and bear fruit, even in old age. We stay fresh and green each new day with Jesus. Maybe you feel like your sin has destroyed so many years of your life, but take heart! Psalm 90:15 includes the prayer that God would "make us glad for as many days as you have afflicted us, for as many years as we have seen trouble," and the promise that God will restore "the years the locusts have eaten" (Joel 2:25). Now, in the next chapter, you'll discover one of the best Savior Stories of your life:

You aren't just daily renewed; you are *filled* with the Holy Spirit to experience the incredible life of Christ living through you.

1. Name your Shadow Narrative.
What story do you tell yourself over and over again of how you'll never change or that you'll always be a certain way?

I'm always going to_____

I'm never going to be able to_____

Tell the story of the "old you."

2. Compose your Savior Story of renewal.

3. How do you as a renewed person now live? Compare the old you to the renewed you.

4. Choose an image or object to remind you that you are renewed. Maybe you remember daffodils and spring or purple crocuses that pop up through the snow or some other visual reminder of renewal.

CONFESSION, REPENTANCE, AND RENEWAL

Jesus, right now I confess to You the ways I have sinned against You in the area of _____. I agree with You that this is sin, and I thank You that You have forgiven me. I know that Your Word says You will now cleanse me from all impurity and renew a right spirit within me. God, I desire to repent of these attitudes and behaviors, and I want to go in a new direction.

Help me change anything in my environment that enables or encourages this sin, and help me cut out temptation from my life.

Finally, help me know how to repair any damage my sin has caused. I also thank You that I don't have to live in guilt and shame anymore because "there is no condemnation for those who are in Christ Jesus" (Rom. 8:1). I know You forgive me, so please help me forgive myself.

Please, Jesus, guide me in the "paths of righteousness" and help me become the person I'm supposed to be. Send godly people to surround me, lead me to godly places, and provide all that I need to grow in my relationship with You.

filled

Ephesians 5:1–21

"This, of course, is what it means to be filled with the Holy Spirit—to allow the Holy Spirit to occupy the whole of your personality with the adequacy of Christ. This is the sublime secret of drawing upon the unlimited resources of Deity."

—Major W. Ian Thomas in *The Saving Life of Christ*

A GOAL FOR LIVING

Read Ephesians 5:1–21 and underline all the commands.

Follow God's example, therefore, as dearly loved children and walk in the way of love, just as Christ loved us and gave himself up for us as a fragrant offering and sacrifice to God.

But among you there must not be even a hint of sexual immorality, or of any kind of impurity, or of greed, because these are improper for God's holy people. Nor should there be obscenity, foolish talk or coarse joking, which are out of place, but rather thanksgiving. For of this you can be sure: No immoral, impure or greedy person—such a person is an idolater—has any inheritance in the kingdom of Christ and of God. Let no one deceive you with empty words, for because of such things God's wrath comes on those who are disobedient. Therefore do not be partners with them.

For you were once darkness, but now you are light in the Lord. Live as children of light (for the fruit of the light consists in all goodness, righteousness and truth) and find out what pleases the Lord.

Have nothing to do with the fruitless deeds of darkness, but rather expose them. It is shameful even to mention what the disobedient do in secret. But everything exposed by the light becomes visible—and everything that is illuminated becomes a light. This is why it is said:

"Wake up, sleeper,
   rise from the dead,
   and Christ will shine on you."

Be very careful, then, how you live—not as unwise but as wise, making the most of every opportunity, because the days are evil. Therefore do not be foolish, but understand what the Lord's will is. Do not get drunk on wine, which leads to debauchery. Instead, be filled with the Spirit, speaking to one another with psalms, hymns, and songs from the Spirit. Sing and make music from your heart to the Lord, always giving thanks to God the Father for everything, in the name of our Lord Jesus Christ.

Submit to one another out of reverence for Christ.

As we begin our study of this first part of chapter 5, let's consider some of the beautiful phrases before we isolate the most important verb. I teach my Advanced Writing students to craft a Personal Mission Statement to use in their professional packets and in job interviews. The Personal Mission Statement is a two-sentence summary of what they devote themselves to in their career, their professional goals, and the way they intend to achieve those goals. I write on the board:

I devote myself to_____.

My goals include_____ that I will achieve by_____.

Some students report that composing their Personal Mission Statement ranks as the single hardest writing task of their lives. Ephesians 5:1–21 functions as a Personal Mission Statement for Christians. We might say, *We devote ourselves to Jesus. We intend to then live a life of love, as children of light, who make the most of every opportunity that we achieve by being filled with the Holy Spirit.*

Write down some characteristics of someone who

Lives a life of love:

Lives as a child of light:

Makes the most of every opportunity:

To aid in composing this list, you might also think about the opposite of each category. For example, we can live a life of love, or we can live a life of selfishness and hate. We can live as a child of light (in all goodness, righteousness, and truth) or we can live in the sin Paul describes.

Paul instructs us to avoid even a "hint" of sexual immorality. A child of the light flees from even a "hint" of sin. Think about what it means to "make the most of every opportunity" and confess the opposite: laziness, a lack of discernment, wasting time, and all the ways we let wonderful opportunities—however we define those—pass us by.

But in the Personal Mission Statement activity, I ask students to tell me *how* they will do the things they want to do. So how will we live a life of love, as a child of light, who makes the most of every opportunity?

And now we come to the operative verb in Ephesians 5. We live this way because we are "filled"—controlled and empowered by—the Holy Spirit.

Chapter 5 of Ephesians continues this theme of renewal and of casting off the old flesh, but we find a curious and often misunderstood command to "be filled with the Spirit" (v. 18) that Paul contrasts with the command "do not get drunk on wine." What a strange comparison! I clearly remember the year I learned about the Spirit-filled life in my time growing as a Christian through the ministry of Cru and in my new church. I learned something astonishing: God's Spirit indwells every believer, but not all Christians allow themselves to be controlled and empowered by the Holy Spirit.

When I examined this passage from Ephesians for the first time, I wondered why Paul would contrast intoxication to being filled with God's Spirit. The girls in our Bible study reported what they knew about intoxication and how it changes your speech and behavior. Intoxication overtakes your brain and your personality. It causes you to do things you wouldn't normally do. We wondered if that was Paul's aim—to invite us to experience the control of the Holy Spirit so we would no longer be the same ordinary people. The Holy Spirit would overtake our lives like intoxication.

I had many questions about this indwelling Holy Spirit. What was He doing in me? How would I know He was working? How could I "be filled" as Paul commands?

Greek scholars have noted the verb *filled* means the sense of the Holy Spirit continually controlling us. In fact, Paul uses a present imperative verb meaning, "Be constantly, moment by moment, controlled by the Holy Spirit."[1] I understood the verb *filled* to refer to something more closely related to the verb "overcome with" or "controlled by," as when one is "filled with rage" or "overcome with passion." This made sense when I considered the comparison to intoxication. Paul is commanding us to allow the Holy Spirit to control and overcome us, causing us to do things we wouldn't do on our own, with power we don't always realize we have, in places we wouldn't normally go.

But how does this work? If I asked Jesus to control me by the Holy Spirit—to direct and empower my whole life—would He answer that prayer?

Dr. Bill Bright's article "Have You Made the Wonderful Discovery of the Spirit-Filled Life?" explains what it means to invite the Holy Spirit to daily empower and control our lives.[2] Instead of remaining self-directed and self-empowered, we could confess any known sin and ask the Holy Spirit to fill us (direct, empower) afresh. We can choose to ask God to take over the control center of our life, to put Him in charge as Lord of every area, and to surrender completely to this direction. Dr. Bright continues his explanation:

> A Christian who is controlled and empowered by the Holy Spirit of God draws upon the unlimited resources of God's love and power and lives in the strength of the living Christ. He understands and believes God's Word, and his interests and ambitions are centered around and subject to the perfect will of God. Spiritually, he is alive. He is rejoicing in the Lord and bearing fruit for our Savior because he is allowing the Holy Spirit to have unhindered control of his life.[3]

Think about the "unlimited resources of God" and what it would mean to allow the Holy Spirit to "have unhindered control of [your] life." The command to "be filled" is a command to empty our lives of self-direction and self-effort and to fill ourselves with God's direction and God's power for living. So many Christians miss this most essential part of the Christian life. We live defeated, exhausted, and confused lives because we miss the Spirit-filled life. We live with a lack of intimacy with Jesus with little desire to worship or read God's Word.

We are Christians, yes, but we aren't "in step" and "filled" with the Holy Spirit. Being filled doesn't mean we ask for *more* of the Holy Spirit or to receive Him as if for the first time. The Holy Spirit is already fully present within us, and we have all of Him that we'll ever have when we pray to receive Christ. But while we possess all of the Holy Spirit, we often fail to provide Him unhindered access to every area of our lives. We don't surrender full control of our lives. We aren't living in radical dependence on His guidance and power. Our self-interest and self-effort, as well as our sin, keep us from experiencing the Spirit-filled life.

Right now, we can confess self-sufficiency and began to depend more and more on the Holy Spirit within us. The Holy Spirit enables us to do what seems impossible in the list of commands in Ephesians 5—that continues with the much-discussed commands to wives and husbands in verses 22–33. Submitting to one another may seem *impossible*—like this surrendering of all your rights means an unnatural death to self. But with the Holy Spirit, all things are possible.

Look again at the list and add on any other characteristics of someone walking closely with Jesus, filled with His spirit.

Look again at chapter 5 and write down how someone filled with God's Spirit behaves. The list is started for you:

They live as children of light—in goodness, righteousness, and truth.

They find out what pleases the Lord in every situation.

They expose deeds of darkness in whatever way that applies to their lives.

They live careful, wise lives that make the most of every opportunity.

They _____ what the Lord's will is.

They _____ that praise Him.

They _____ in everything.

They _____ to one another.

As you think about this list, we can ask God for His power and wisdom for every characteristic you noted above. We can thank God that He empowers us to understand His will, to speak in ways that praise Him, to give thanks in everything, and to submit to one another. We can depend upon the Holy Spirit to empower and direct us into these commands.

Let's look at our list of questions to see if we can gain more understanding into this strange verb, *filled*. When you see that verb, remember to think of the words "controlled, empowered, and overcome" to help us gain the right sense of the word.

Who fills us?

When are we filled?

How are we filled?

Where is this filling happening?

What's different about filled people?

Why is He filling us?

UNHINDERED POWER

When I think about being "filled with the Holy Spirit" and the complete takeover by something akin to intoxication, I think of the word "surrender." I know that my sin and self-directed, self-effort kind of living thwarts the power of the Holy Spirit, so I pray that God would help me die to myself and live a crucified life. In Galatians 2:20, Paul declares, "I have been crucified with Christ and I no longer live, but Christ lives in me. The life I now live in the body, I live by faith in the Son of God, who loved me and gave himself for me."

For the last twenty years, that verse operates as my "life verse." The most powerful movements of God in my life occurred during the seasons when I gave up my rights to myself and surrendered myself, as completely as I knew how, to God's plans for my life. When I studied people who seemed to have a special sense of God's power, provision, and fruitfulness, I discovered that they live surrendered lives where they "die to themselves." They often say, like Jesus Himself, "not my will but Yours," Lord. I ask the Holy Spirit each new day to help me "die to myself."

Do you have a Savior Story of when you "died to yourself"? Read 1 Corinthians 6:19–20: "You are not your own; you were bought at a price." What does it mean that "you are not your own"?

My Savior Story of surrender occurred on a country road in Saline, Michigan. I imagined God asking me the question, "Will you live the life I ask you to?"

I was honest with God on that country road. I was living in the Shadow Narrative that God had ruined my life. I felt angry and hopeless because the life I had planned for myself wasn't happening. To top it off, I felt guilty for feeling so depressed. After all, I had a husband and a new baby. I had shelter and food and a thousand other things to make my life comfortable.

But I wanted a different life, one of wealth and fame and prestige. I didn't want to be home with a baby. I didn't want to have a life of vocational ministry that included raising financial support for the rest of my life. I didn't want to live in Michigan where it snowed until April and my hands were so chapped from the cold they cracked and bled every morning. I told God that everything I wanted for myself hadn't happened and never would happen. I felt ugly, poor, and useless.

But then the question: "Will you live the life I ask you to?"

I thought about Jesus and His love for me. I thought about His goodness and power. I thought about whether or not I would allow Him to truly be the Lord of my life. That day on that country road, I surrendered everything—as best as I knew how—into the hands of God. I said, "Yes, Lord. I will live the life You ask me to, even if it means I'm ugly, poor, and useless. Even if it means living here for the rest of my life. Even if it means I'll suffer, I'll still follow You."

My life changed after that day. The depression lifted so quickly that my therapist said to "mark the day as an intervention of God" because something healed in me. I felt the filling of the Holy Spirit who would then empower me and enable me to live a life I couldn't live in my own strength.

A professor at Penn State recently shared the perfect image for understanding surrender and how to think about becoming an unhindered channel of the Holy Spirit's filling power. The professor explained that, in ecology, "nurse log" refers to a tree that falls to the forest floor.

Picture an enormous tree surrendering and falling down. When it rests on the forest floor in that fallen position, it becomes a nurse log and begins caring for all the living things around it. It provides nutrients as it decays. It provides more light to shine on others in its new position. According to the professor, "When a nurse log falls down, it allows more light to emanate into the space where it once stood." She explains the analogy to a surrendered life and writes,

> As you fall, you illuminate more; as you decay, you bestow an unending and ample supply of nutrients and energy so that new saplings can form and mature to their intended height and beauty. Interestingly, when a tree is standing, only about 5% of it is living material. But when it falls, it transforms completely from a tree to a log. The tree resurrects into a fresh life and now contains five times as much living matter than before. The tree is utterly altered into beautiful, rich, organic material—ready to spawn a new generation through the sacrifice of its body.
>
> Nurse logs not only give water and nutrients, but they offer disease protection . . . [and] provide a protective barrier from these pathogens, and increase seedling survivorship.[4]

As the professor and I discussed the surrendered life, it amazed us that when we "die to self" like the nurse log, we're five times more useful, and we leave our environment richer, more protected, and with a greater legacy for the next generation. Sure, we can stand tall and take up all the light, but when we fall, we illuminate Jesus. As we decay, we help so many others.

The image of the nurse log is helpful when we consider surrender and the Spirit-filled life.

Now that we've looked at the Spirit-filled life for a few days, let's see if we can answer these questions:

What's the connection between being surrendered and being "filled with the Spirit"?

How would you teach someone to surrender to God?

What are the indicators that we're filled with the Spirit? When we're filled with God's Spirit, we long to read God's Word, to spend time in prayer, and to connect with God's people. We're sensitive to sin. We're eager to have our life bring attention to Jesus and not ourselves. We want to talk to others about Jesus. We find ourselves doing loving acts of service. We find ourselves accepting others, meeting their needs above our own. We find ourselves speaking words of wisdom and using our gifts to bless people. When we're filled with God's Spirit, people experience blessing in our presence because they sense Jesus Christ.

Spirit-filled people demonstrate the fruit of the Spirit in speech, attitude, and behavior.

How do we recognize when we're not filled with the Spirit? Scripture says that the works of the flesh are "obvious." We all, to some extent, suffer from the works of the flesh described in Galatians 5:19. While we may not be practicing witchcraft or engaging in sexually immoral acts, we might have thoughts, attitudes, and actions that fall under these broad categories. We might have lust in our heart, or might feed the flesh by the movies, books, or television shows we choose.

What are some of your personal markers that help you know when you're living as one filled with the Spirit? What are some of your personal indicators that alert you when you're not?

Give some examples of what it feels like (or what you can imagine it feels like) to be "filled with the Spirit."

WHAT IS THE HOLY SPIRIT DOING?

As we think more about the command in Ephesians 5 to "be filled," we might still have a limited view of what the Holy Spirit does in us and in the world. Let's examine what the Bible teaches about the Holy Spirit. The most important teaching on the Holy Spirit comes from John 14 through the words of Jesus. He says:

> If you love me, keep my commands. And I will ask the Father, and he will give you another advocate to help you and be with you forever—the Spirit of truth. The world cannot accept him, because it neither sees him nor knows him. But you know him, for he lives with you and will be in you. (vv. 15–17)

And a few verses later, Jesus says that "the Advocate, the Holy Spirit, whom the Father will send in my name, will teach you all things and will remind you of everything I have said to you" (v. 26).

Write down how Jesus describes the Holy Spirit above.

Now look at some of the ways Scripture further describes the Holy Spirit. If you like, you can note by each item in the list whether this activity reflects the Holy Spirit as Teacher, Advocate, Helper, or Comforter.

Intercedes for us when we don't know what to pray (Rom. 8:26–27)

Teaches us God's truth (John 14:26; 1 Cor. 2:13)

Provides discernment (1 Cor. 2:14)

Gives power in our weakness (Rom.8:26)

Empowers us for ministry (Isa. 11:2; Acts 1:8)

Gives courage and boldness to act and speak (Acts 4:31)

Compels us to action (Acts 20:22)

Leads us (Matt. 4:1; Rom. 8:14; Acts 16:6–7)

Speaks through us and give us words to say (Matt. 10:20; Mark 13:11; Luke 12:12)

Gives wisdom and understanding (Col. 1:9)

Is a Spirit of truth (1 John 4:6)

Makes us overflow with hope (Rom. 15:13)

Convicts us of sin (John 16:8)

Comes to us in an unlimited way (John 3:34)

Produces new life in us (John 6:63; Titus 3:5)

Fills us with joy (Luke 10:21; 1 Thess. 1:6)

Gives spiritual gifts to us (1 Cor. 12)

Brings freedom (2 Cor. 3:17)

Bears witness that we belong to God as sons and daughters (Rom. 8:15–16)

Sanctifies us (Rom. 15:16; 2 Thess. 2:13)

Brings unity (Eph. 4:3)

Produces the fruit of the Spirit (Gal. 5:22)

Gives us songs to sing (Eph. 5:19; Col. 3:16)

Pours God's love into our hearts (Rom. 5:5)

Brings peace as we allow our minds to be governed by Him (Rom. 8:6)

Puts to death our sinful behavior (Rom. 8:13)

Can be quenched (1 Thess. 5:19)

Can be grieved by our sin (Eph. 4:30)

As we examine the Scriptures, we can summarize all the roles of the Holy Spirit and remember that He always helps, empowers, teaches, and reminds us that we belong to God. I recently wrote this in my journal to summarize what I was learning about the Holy Spirit filling me. *He fills us to say and do things we normally wouldn't do, in places we normally wouldn't go, with people we normally wouldn't know, with resources we didn't know we had.*

Reflect: What roles of the Holy Spirit most intrigue you? Which ones would you like to learn more about?

WEEK 6 | DAY 4

IMAGINING THE SPIRIT-FILLED LIFE

As we review yesterday's list of what the Holy Spirit does, we may be inspired to think more fully about what it would mean to live a Spirit-led instead of a self-directed life. Can you imagine what your life would look like if you daily lived in the power of the Holy Spirit?

What would a day look like that was governed by the Holy Spirit?

When I imagine the Spirit-filled life, I think of Jesus as the leader, the captain, and even like He's a big boat. I'm just resting in the boat, *along for the ride.* I'm swept up in Him, following wherever that current takes me. But then, more often than not, this current takes me to people who need to know Jesus.

Other times when I think of the Spirit-filled life, I see someone standing up and encouraging people, like Peter, who after receiving power from the Holy Spirit, "stood up . . . raised his voice, and addressed the crowd" (Acts 2:14). The image in my mind is someone who stands up, raises her voice, and addresses a crowd.

What pictures come to your mind?

Pastor Jim Cymbala writes in *Fresh Power*:

> I want to be totally yielded to God, don't you? I don't want to live half full; I
> want to experience what it means to be full of the Holy Spirit in the way God
> intended. He promised that through the gospel and the Spirit's anointing, our
> lives could be used . . . to bring blessing and hope to multitudes. The thought
> of that means far more to me than any worldly honor or achievement. I don't
> want a title: I don't want to be famous or meet some earthly dignitary; I don't
> want to be rich. I just want God to clothe me with his Spirit so I can affect
> people for Christ.[5]

When Cymbala thinks about his life, he's not thinking about honors or achievement or some kind of meeting with important people. He's thinking about being
clothed with the Holy Spirit to "bring blessing and hope to the multitudes." If you
review the list of the Holy Spirit's activity, what is most exciting is that it includes
this primary role of *power for ministry*.

I memorized Acts 1:8 and quoted it as I began to talk to more and more people
about Jesus: "But you will receive power when the Holy Spirit comes on you; and
you will be my witnesses in Jerusalem, and in all Judea and Samaria, and to the
ends of the earth." I noted, like Cymbala, that the Holy Spirit comes in power
to enable proclamation and widespread ministry. My mentor and I observed the
ever-increasing ripples of Holy Spirit–power for witnessing; it begins nearby in Jerusalem and extends out first to Judea, then wider still to far-off Samaria, and then
to the very ends of the earth. We asked ourselves, "Where is our Jerusalem?"

While being mindful of Holy Spirit power to bring blessing and hope to your
"Jerusalem," read with joy Acts 17:26–27 and how God chose the time and exact
place where you and I live for a reason: "[God] marked out their appointed times
in history and the boundaries of their lands. God did this so that they would seek
him and perhaps reach out for him and find him, though he is not far from any
one of us."

My Jerusalem, then, was first my home and neighborhood, then my workplace, then my larger city. Focusing on my boundaries of my neighborhood, and being filled with God's Spirit to bring blessing, hope, and proclamation, changed everything about my life when I exclusively devoted myself to this little "Jerusalem." For years, our family hosted Saturday morning pancake breakfasts for the neighbors, launched a walk-to-school campaign, designed a Monday Night Neighborhood fitness group, and planned many social events for neighbors in order to bless them and talk to them about Jesus.

Where is your "Jerusalem"?

What people come to mind who don't know Jesus where you live, work, and spend most of your time? What are their greatest needs?

If you really believed that the Holy Spirit gives you power to be a witness, how does that change how you go about your ordinary day?

Jennifer Rich writes a beautiful testimony of the Spirit-filled life below. Jennifer was the first person I ever heard use that term when I was a graduate student, and she continues to inspire me with her dependence on the Holy Spirit.

My mother led me to Christ when I was ten years old, and I have attended church all my life; yet, for many years, I harbored a nagging fear that my relationship with God was missing something. I knew that I was a sinner saved by Jesus Christ, but I had no idea how to live out the Christian life. I strove to follow Him but often felt like a failure—carrying an increasing burden of guilt and shame, feeling that I couldn't measure up to what I thought was the model Christian life. Right before freshman year at Michigan State University, I finally cried out to God in prayer: If indeed I was missing something about Him, would He please show me?

During freshman year, I got involved with the student ministry of Cru (formerly Campus Crusade for Christ). My understanding of God's love expanded greatly, but it wasn't until sophomore year that I began to hear others mention the "Spirit-filled life." I was so curious about it. My Bible study leader at the time discerned that I was trying to live out faith by my own power and strength. She encouraged me to instead ask the Holy Spirit for help to live the Christian life. I remember being struck by the truth that God wanted to be my Helper (John 16:7–15), and that apart from Him I could do nothing (John 15:5)—that moment became a profound life-changing experience! I finally understood that I didn't have to (and for that matter, couldn't) strive to be good; rather, the Holy Spirit would work goodness through me as I submitted to His authority and power in my life.

Twenty-seven years ago, I first understood that Jesus sent the Holy Spirit to help us. Since then, I have learned that the fruit of the Spirit (Gal. 5:22–23) is supernatural and not something I can produce on my own. Apart from Him, I cannot love others well, be patient with my children, or exercise self-control. Indeed, the Spirit-filled life is one of the most significant theological realities I have ever known. A recent, particularly desertlike season of life has been teaching me to lean into the Spirit more than ever. He sustains me when I am inclined toward fear and anxiety. But as I trust and abide in Him daily, the Spirit continues to conform and shape my heart, bearing His fruit in my life.

WEEK 6 | DAY 5

WRITING YOUR STORY

1. Name your Shadow Narrative.
What story do you tell about the boring, frustrated, unfruitful, try-harder kind of Christian life? Or compose the story of your self-directed, self-empowered life. What has this life been like for you?

2. Compose your Savior Story of filled. When did you feel empowered by the Holy Spirit to do something you normally would not do?

3. Compare and contrast: How does someone live differently who is "filled with the Spirit"?

4. Choose an image or object to remind you that you are surrendered and now filled.

CONFESSION, REPENTANCE, AND RENEWAL

When I was twenty-four-years old, I read a book that powerfully affected my life. It was *A Woman after God's Own Heart*, by Elizabeth George.[6] I wanted to walk closely with Jesus, but I wasn't sure how. I wanted to surrender to Him completely. I wanted to know how to build my adult life. In this book, I discovered a prayer that Elizabeth George wrote on the front page of her own Bible written by Betty Scott Stam, a China Inland Mission Worker. Stam's daily prayer was this:

> Lord, I give up all my own plans and purposes, all my own desire and hopes, and I accept Thy will for my life. I give myself, my time, my all, utterly to Thee to be Thine forever. Fill me and seal me with Thy Holy Spirit. Use me as Thou wilt, send me where Thou wilt, work out Thy whole will in my life at any cost, now and forever.[7]

In the margin of the book, I wrote that this was the "hardest prayer I'll ever pray." I asked God to help me pray a prayer of confession and surrender to experience the control and empowerment of the Holy Spirit in increasing measure. From this moment on, incredible, supernatural moments filled my life as I cooperated with Jesus to lead others to Christ.

Offer to God a prayer of surrender. Confess any known sin and ask the Holy Spirit to fill you. By faith, you can believe that this has happened. By faith, you can be assured that the power of the Holy Spirit is operating with you. This is pleasing to God.

Remember Hebrews 11:6: "Without faith it is impossible to please God, because anyone who comes to him must believe that he exists and that he rewards those who earnestly seek him." God will answer prayers that are prayed "according to His will." In 1 John 5:14, we read, "This is the confidence we have in approaching God: that if we ask anything according to his will, he hears us."

God hears your prayer to be filled with the Spirit of God because it's a command in Scripture. He hears and He answers, and you can know that you are filled with the Holy Spirit today.

proclaiming

Ephesians 6:10–20

"But during the night an angel of the Lord opened the doors of
the jail and brought them out. 'Go, stand in the temple courts,'
he said, 'and tell the people all about this new life.'"

—The angel to Peter in Acts 5:19–20

"To be a soul winner is the happiest thing in this world."

—Charles Spurgeon

PROTECTION

Read Ephesians 6:10–20.

Finally, be strong in the Lord and in his mighty power. Put on the full armor of God, so that you can take your stand against the devil's schemes. For our struggle is not against flesh and blood, but against the rulers, against the authorities, against the powers of this dark world and against the spiritual forces of evil in the heavenly realms.

Therefore put on the full armor of God, so that when the day of evil comes, you may be able to stand your ground, and after you have done everything, to stand. Stand firm then, with the belt of truth buckled around your waist, with the breastplate of righteousness in place, and with your feet fitted with the readiness that comes from the gospel of peace. In addition to all this, take up the shield of faith, with which you can extinguish all the flaming arrows of the evil one. Take the helmet of salvation and the sword of the Spirit, which is the word of God.

And pray in the Spirit on all occasions with all kinds of prayers and requests. With this in mind, be alert and always keep on praying for all the Lord's people. Pray also for me, that whenever I speak, words may be given me so that I will fearlessly make known the mystery of the gospel, for which I am an ambassador in chains. Pray that I may declare it fearlessly, as I should.

Underline the commands in this passage and list out each piece of armor you discover.

Reading Ephesians 6:10–20 fortifies me every time I read it. For the majority of the book of Ephesians, Paul teaches us how *to think rightly of ourselves*; we are included, chosen, and seated. He teaches us *how to enjoy Jesus and draw our energy from God to live*; we are strengthened, renewed, and filled. But in Ephesians 6, Paul teaches us about *our mission as long as we remain on earth.*

What is this mission?

We are engaged in spiritual battle as we proclaim the gospel to all nations.

First let's look at what we learn about the enemy based on this passage.

> *Who is this enemy?*
> *What is this enemy like?*
> *Why do we have an enemy?*
> *Where does this enemy operate?*

How does this enemy attack?

When does this enemy attack?

One way I understand how the enemy attacks is by examining what each type of armor works to neutralize. For example, we need the breastplate of righteousness to fight the accusations of the enemy and his desire that we live in condemnation, shame, and guilt. Christ's righteousness protects us from these assaults.

Consider the following:

What does the belt of truth protect us from?

What does the breastplate of righteousness guard us from?

What do the shoes of the gospel of peace protect us from?

What does the shield of faith do?

What does the helmet of salvation protect us from?

What does the sword of the Spirit (God's Word) do?

Which weapon does each attack need?

1. The devil's schemes (cunning arts, deceit, trickery, traps) require_____

2. The devil's lies require_____

3. The devil's accusations require_____

4. The devil's discord and harassment require _____

5. The devil's use of doubt and uncertainty requires_____

6. The devil's attacks in all forms require_____

I think about the enemy of our souls who operates with clever scheming, lies, accusations, harassment, planting doubts, and attacks in various forms. I think of the "flaming arrows" of discouragement. He seeks to "steal and kill and destroy" (John 10:10). In 1 Peter 5:8, we learn that our "enemy the devil prowls around like a roaring lion looking for someone to devour."

The enemy of our souls especially desires to thwart the advancement of God's kingdom. Satan blocks the way (see 1 Thess. 2:18). He also works to "[blind] the minds of unbelievers, so that they cannot see the light of the gospel that displays the glory of Christ, who is the image of God" (2 Cor. 4:4). Satan, finally, loves to steal God's words from our hearts as soon as we hear them (Mark 4:15).

As I think about our assignment from Jesus, the Great Commission, I have learned more and more how much Satan works to actively undermine God's plan for us to "go into all the world and preach the gospel to all creation" (Mark 16:15). In Matthew 28:18–20, we read it more fully: "Then Jesus came to them and said, 'All authority in heaven and on earth has been given to me. Therefore go and make disciples of all nations, baptizing them in the name of the Father and of the Son and of the Holy Spirit, and teaching them to obey everything I have commanded you. And surely I am with you always, to the very end of the age.'"

We need the armor of God because of the battle mission assigned to us: We move out into the battle each new day *protected and proclaiming*. Satan, however, works against us to thwart us and silence us. When I joined the staff of Cru, the person doing my interview said, "Now it's as if you have an X on your back like you're a target for the enemy." He explained that when we move into our roles of evangelism and discipleship, spiritual warfare increases considerably.

But I wasn't scared; I was *excited*. I knew that Satan was a defeated foe, a yappy dog on a short leash, and subject to the power and authority of Jesus Christ. While God might allow Satan and his demons to harass me, they could never harm my soul. But I didn't want to be foolish. Ephesians 6 showcases a picture of the enemy as organized and strategic. The devil schemes against us, lays traps, and works to discourage and defeat us especially as we advance God's kingdom.

Ephesians 6, then, teaches us to "be strong in the Lord and in His mighty power."

I thought of a question this morning that brought conviction to my soul. *How do I seek to be strong in things other than the Lord and His mighty power?*

How would you answer? How do you seek to be strong in things other than the Lord and His mighty power?

A PERSONAL PRAYER FOR PAUL

Many readers of Ephesians 6 miss the beautiful moment when, after outlining the armor of God, Paul requests something very special. I've read this section of Ephesians more times than I can count, and this year I noticed a sentence I had overlooked.

In verses 19–20, Paul asks for prayer for *himself*. "Pray also for me." What would he ask for? I couldn't wait to read on. Paul could ask his readers to pray for *anything*. What would he request? What was most on his mind? Maybe he would ask for freedom, for a wife, for more resources, or for better health. Maybe he would ask for more joy, more peace, or more comfort, or a thousand other things related to personal happiness.

But no. Paul asks for none of these things. Guess what he asks for—see what the singular focus of his heart was as he concludes this powerful letter. He appeals for this:

> Pray also for me, that whenever I speak, words may be given me so that I will fearlessly make known the mystery of the gospel, for which I am an ambassador in chains. Pray that I may declare it fearlessly, as I should.

He asks for *words*.

Fearless words to make known the mystery of the gospel.

Some translations use the verb *proclaim*, and the Greek translation of those phrases "words may be given me" and "declare it fearlessly" mean that Paul asks for *open, unreserved, clear, confident, cheerful, courageous* speaking. The verb here, "proclaim," means also a *bold, assured, and free way of talking.*[1]

Paul requests personal prayer only a few times throughout his letters, and besides asking just once for others to pray for his safety and favor in Romans 15:30–31 and deliverance from evil in 2 Thessalonians 3:2, he asks *three more times for prayer* about proclaiming the gospel. He asks this: "Pray for us, too, that God may open a door for our message, so that we may proclaim the mystery of Christ, for which I am in chains" (Col. 4:3). Paul adds a follow-up request in the next verse: "Pray that I may proclaim it clearly, as I should" (Col. 4:4). Then in 2 Thessalonians 3:1, Paul asks for prayer that the message of Christ "may spread rapidly."

As Paul inhabited his included, chosen, seated, strengthened, renewed, and filled identity, he now clearly understood his mission. He *proclaims*. Despite having undergone many hardships and expecting to encounter more, Paul penned some of the most beautiful words in the New Testament, found in the book of Acts. He writes, "I consider my life worth nothing to me; my only aim is to finish the race and complete the task the Lord Jesus has given me—the task of testifying to the good news of God's grace" (20:24).

Could we ever say, like Paul, that we consider our lives worth nothing to us? That our *only aim* in life was to testify to the good news?

What do you think Paul experienced in Jesus Christ that would cause him to write these words in Acts 20:24?

Read Paul's prayer again from Ephesians 6:19–20 to learn more about Paul and Jesus.

> Pray also for me, that whenever I speak, words may be given me so that I will fearlessly make known the mystery of the gospel, for which I am an ambassador in chains. Pray that I may declare it fearlessly, as I should.

What do you notice about this prayer?

We can also shape this prayer into a life mission. **How would you word these thoughts to your own mission?**

I love that Paul finds strength, not in his understanding or his feelings of peace and safety. In fact, understanding everything about Jesus and feeling easy and peaceful are not conditions for sharing the gospel. We proclaim despite these realities in the power of the Holy Spirit.

YOUR OWN PURPOSE AND PRAYER

What if we prayed Ephesians 6:18–19 for ourselves? What if we asked God and believed He would grant us this request, that *He might open our mouths boldly to proclaim*? If you know anything about Paul's mouth, you might find such a request deeply ironic. After all, Paul used his mouth for some terrible things (maybe you can relate! I certainly can).

He also kept silent when he could have intervened in the stoning of Stephen (Acts 7:57–8:1). While the crowd was "yelling at the top of their voices" in a riotous rush to stone God's servant, Stephen, Scripture records that Paul (called Saul before his conversion to Christ) stood there and allowed those people to lay their clothes at his feet as a symbol of his authority. As Stephen was stoned in front of the crowd, Acts 8:1 records, "And Saul approved of their killing him." We learn how Saul lived as one "breathing out murderous threats against the Lord's disciples."

But when Jesus gets ahold of Saul and transforms him, this man's mouth begins to boldly proclaim Jesus (Acts 9:27–28). In Acts 9, in fact, we read that after Paul met Jesus on the road to Damascus, he was struck blind. When Ananias comes three days later and prays for him, he receives his sight again; he was baptized; eats some food; and then Scripture says, "And immediately he began to proclaim Jesus in the synagogues, saying, 'He is the Son of God'" (Acts 9:20 NASB).

Can you imagine what people thought? In Acts 9, we have the record of their words. We read, "All those who heard him were astonished and asked, 'Isn't he the man who raised havoc in Jerusalem among those who call on this name?'" (v. 21). Paul knows how people feel about him—and all the terrible history they know about his life—but he changes that Shadow Narrative into the Savior Story. In Galatians 1:13–16, he writes,

> For you have heard of my previous way of life in Judaism, how intensely I persecuted the church of God and tried to destroy it. I was advancing in Judaism beyond many of my own age among my people and was extremely zealous for the traditions of my fathers. But when God, who set me apart from my mother's womb and called me by his grace, was pleased to reveal his Son in me so that I might preach him among the Gentiles, my immediate response was not to consult any human being.

Note Paul's thinking here. He recounts the Shadow Narrative (his previous way of life) and the Savior Story of chosen (set apart from birth) to now use his mouth to "preach him." During his final imprisonment, Paul still understands the Shadow Narrative turned into the Savior Story. He writes near the end of his life in 1 Timothy 1:13–16 the following:

> Even though I was once a blasphemer and a persecutor and a violent man, I was shown mercy because I acted in ignorance and unbelief. The grace of our Lord was poured out on me abundantly, along with the faith and love that are in Christ Jesus.

> Here is a trustworthy saying that deserves full acceptance: Christ Jesus came into the world to save sinners—of whom I am the worst. But for that very reason I was shown mercy so that in me, the worst of sinners, Christ Jesus might display his immense patience as an example for those who would believe in him and receive eternal life.

The Greek translation of "worst" of sinners means that Paul believed he was the highest, chief, first, and best sinner. In other words, if you feel like you are the worst sinner ever, Paul has you beat. Paul carries that Shadow Narrative of what his mouth used to do, but he blends it into his Savior Story of how his mouth now proclaims truth. Paul's statement is a good place to begin your own personal testimony of God's work. You might even fill in the blanks with your own name:

Even though I was once a _____ and a _____
I was shown mercy.

One of my favorite Savior Stories of seeing God transform a woman's words comes from my dear friend JoAnn Foley-DeFiore. She writes her story of God redeeming her words and giving back her dream of singing.

When I was a little girl, I always had a dream of being a singer on a stage in the lights. However, nothing in my life led to the fruition of this vision. I never lost the hope, though, and during the difficult times in my early twenties and thirties, such as sexual assault, dating violence, and the death of my best friend, my mind would wander to this daydream as a form of solace, a refuge. Since I did not yet have a relationship with Jesus or a church family at that time, I would often sing for hours at home for comfort.

In my thirties and early forties, I was still seeking something spiritual, and found myself in a yoga and meditation group, where we did chanting quite a bit. I began to chant more and more often, even at home on my own. Then when I was forty-three, I gave my life to Jesus Christ and that changed everything! For several years, I could not sing; maybe God wanted to purify my voice from its other past uses. Moreover, I had lost the desire to sing. Maybe I did not need to sing. I had Jesus now and He is my solace, my comfort, my sanctuary.

A few years later, something astonishing happened. God planted that dream of singing into my heart again, and within a few weeks, I was asked to sing with our Saturday evening worship team. Now, God has fulfilled the dream He gave me. I am finally singing on the stage with the lights, but now it all belongs to Him. He changed my voice so I could sing His praises, sing of His comfort, and sing that He is our refuge.

List out in confession and repentance any sins of speech that come to mind. I think about these "sins of speech" throughout Scripture: lying (Prov. 6:17), slander and gossip (Lev. 19:16), flattery (Ps. 12:3), boasting (Ps. 12:3), arguing (Phil. 2:14), complaining (Phil. 2:14), obscenities (Eph. 5:4), coarse joking (Eph. 5:4), cursing people (Rom. 3:13–14), stirring up controversy (Prov. 6:19), and betraying a confidence (Prov. 11:13).

I currently pray about any ways I stir up controversy, complain, or gossip. I desire for Jesus to renew and redeem, to restore and rehabilitate this mouth of mine. What if I used my mouth for thanksgiving, praise, and proclamation instead?

Let's go back to our questions about our verbs:

Who proclaims?

What do I proclaim?

When do I proclaim it?

Why do I proclaim it?

Where do I proclaim it?

How do I proclaim it?

As you've considered these questions, you might start here: What's the first story that comes to mind about what Christ has accomplished in you?

WEEK 7 | DAY 4

THE NEW STORY OF YOUR MOUTH

For the past forty years, God has been teaching me about my words and how to use them both in writing and speaking. I find it fascinating that when Jesus walked the earth, He often healed people who could not speak (e.g., Matt. 12:22, 15:30; Mark 7:31–37). Isn't it interesting that demons made people unable to speak? That Satan stole their words? And when God heals the people who could not speak, they then praise God with their mouths. I just love that. I love that God heals and redeems our words.

When I first knew I belonged to God as a twelve-year-old, I began the journey of telling others what Jesus was accomplishing in me. I didn't know how to "share the gospel"; instead, my message was like the healed blind man who has no sophisticated theology or deep understanding of God. He says, "One thing I do know. I was blind but now I see!" (John 9:25).

In college, as people noticed my rededication to Jesus (and that my foul language ceased), I shared poems and journal entries with the girls in my hall all about what Jesus was doing—how He cleansed me from sin and was now guiding my life. I wanted to share with those girls more fully about what I had experienced, so I ordered the *Billy Graham Christian Worker's Handbook*.[2] I memorized the "Steps to Peace with God" so I could better explain the gospel to my college friends.

I learned how to talk about God's plan for peace and new life (John 3:16), the problem of sin (Rom. 3:23), the remedy of Jesus dying on the cross (1 Peter 2:24), and our response of receiving the free gift of salvation (John 1:12). And I recalled my years of Vacation Bible School and church youth group that taught me to admit, repent, believe, receive—meaning I admit I'm a sinner, agree to turn from my sin, believe in Christ's death on the cross, and receive Jesus in my heart by asking Him to save me.

I wanted to talk about Jesus all the time. As the apostles said, "We cannot help speaking about what we have seen and heard" (Acts 4:20). For the next five years of my life—and primarily through the campus ministry of Cru—I gained training about sharing my faith with others, including preparing a personal testimony (my Savior Story!) and a gospel presentation to lead others to a relationship with Jesus Christ.

I proclaimed wherever, however, whenever, and to whoever would listen. Nothing was more exciting than seeing God supernaturally use me in the lives of other people. Every day became an adventure as I prayed for those around me who didn't know Jesus.

Whenever I feel bored, confused, or unsettled about my faith or life purpose, I go back to the basics of why I'm here, what God is doing in the world, and how He invites me to participate in the kingdom task of proclaiming to others, of preparing the way for the Lord (see Isa.40:3; Matt. 3:3).

I also memorized the goal of 2 Timothy 2:2 where Paul commissions the young Timothy with this mission: "And the things you have heard me say in the presence of many witnesses entrust to reliable people who will also be qualified to teach others."

In other words, whatever you have learned about Jesus, you might pass on to another person.

What emotions come to your mind when you think about God using you to lead another person to Jesus Christ? What do you think it means for you to "entrust" what you have learned about Jesus to other people?

What information do you still need in order to feel confident in sharing the gospel with others and leading them in a prayer of salvation?

Make a list of five to ten people in your life—including family members—who do not yet know Jesus. Begin praying that God "opens a door" for the gospel, provides a "spirit of revelation," and opens their eyes to know Jesus. Look for opportunities to speak about what Jesus has done and is doing in your life (your Savior Stories!).

ALL YOUR WORDS

It seems particularly fitting to end our reading of this letter with the question of what we will proclaim, where, how, and to whom. Over the last few weeks, you've written a collection of Savior Stories of what Jesus has accomplished in you. Think of leaving a legacy of your stories as the writer says in Psalm 102:18: "Let this be written for a future generation, that a people not yet created may praise the LORD." Can you imagine? It's so exciting to think of your life as a catalogue of Savior Stories:

You are included

You are chosen

You are seated

You are strengthened

You are renewed

You are filled

You are proclaiming

I don't believe your Savior Story is just for you alone. I believe God wrote it for you to share with someone else, to bless and help other people. As I began journaling my Savior Stories as a college student and continued for the next years, I often recalled a verse in Isaiah 30:8. It's a command from God that says, "Go now, write it on a tablet for them, inscribe it on a scroll, that for the days to come it may be an everlasting witness." I also listened carefully to the words of Psalm 71:18 where the author writes to God, "Do not forsake me, my God, till I declare your power to the next generation." In Psalm 78:4, the priest writes that he will "tell the next generation the praiseworthy deeds of the LORD, his power, and the wonders he has done." Consult Appendix B for ideas on where you might proclaim your Savior Stories and listen to others share theirs.

Even though I've been involved in public speaking since 1989, have stood in front of college students in classrooms for twenty years, have completed two years of radio interviews, and write every day, I still depend on God's supernatural guidance with my words. I study carefully what the Holy Spirit does through our words, and I gain confidence by believing and relying on helpful Scripture. (See Appendix B for some of these.)

I want to go wherever God wants to send me and say whatever He wants me to say. I don't want my tongue to be what James describes as a "restless evil, full of deadly poison" (James 3:8) or full of the slander, lies, and flattery so warned against in Scripture but most notably in the Proverbs.[3]

I want to be like the woman in Proverbs 31:26: "She speaks with wisdom and faithful instruction is on her tongue."

Take a moment and imagine yourself as speaking with wisdom and faithful instruction to others all day long.

What does God do with our speech? What do we proclaim?

Consider the following verses and answer each question.

• Psalm 40:3: "He put a new song in my mouth, a song of praise to our God. Many will see and fear the LORD and put their trust in him."

Why do you think the writer calls this a "new song"? Imagine what the "old song" was if not one of praising God.

- Psalm 34:1 (NASB): "I will bless the LORD at all times; His praise shall continually be in my mouth."

Have you ever met anyone who continually spoke about Jesus and praised Him? Can you imagine this kind of speech?

- Psalm 51:15: "Open my lips, Lord, and my mouth will declare your praise."

Where do you have "closed lips" that you wish God would open? What environments keep your lips closed?

• Psalm 89:1 (NASB): "I will sing of the lovingkindness of the LORD forever."

Write down three or four sentences as a song of God's lovingkindness.

1. Name your Shadow Narrative.

Part One: Tell the story of your life's words. How have you used your words in the past? How do you use them now in ways that represent your flesh or the old you?

Where have you been "silenced" or have silenced yourself regarding your story of Jesus at work in your life?

2. Compose Your Savior Story of a new song God has put in your mouth.

What is this story? To whom, where, when, and how will you proclaim it?

3. How does a proclaiming person live? Compare the old, silent you to the new, proclaiming you.

4. Choose an image or object to remind you that you are proclaiming.
You might think about the armor of God or how God touches people's mouths before launching them into public ministry (Jer. 1:9; Isa. 6:6–7; Dan. 10:16). Maybe picture a megaphone or even a pen.

CONFESSION, REPENTANCE, AND RENEWAL

As you consider the history of your words—and what you used your mouth for—confess to Jesus any sins of speech or silence that come to mind. Ask Him to redeem and renew this area of your life. Now ask Him how He wants to use your words—either written or spoken—for building His kingdom and helping others grow. Begin dreaming with God where, how, and when you might proclaim in your "Jerusalem."

living your story

"The original, shimmering self gets buried so deep that most of us end up hardly living out of it at all. Instead we live out all the other selves, which we are constantly putting on and taking off like coats and hats against the world's weather."

—Frederick Buechner

"I mean, you can't help nobody if you can't tell them the right story."

—Jack Cash in *Walk the Line*

WEEK 8 | DAY 1

LIVING YOUR STORY TOGETHER

Our study of Ephesians began with the operative word "included." We are included in Christ, together with one another—chosen, seated, strengthened, renewed, filled, and proclaiming—and now we see our Savior Stories as the way we participate in each other's lives.

We have three questions to answer:

1. Do you believe your story is for others?
2. Where are you stuck in your story?
3. How can you continue your story?

Let's tackle the first question.

I know so many of us don't like to speak, write, or do anything that positions us in front of the public. Early in my days of ministry, I noted Psalm 40:10 where David proclaims: "I do not hide your righteousness in my heart; I speak of your faithfulness and your saving help. I do not conceal your love and your faithfulness from the great assembly." When I was tempted to hide away, keep silent, and conceal all that God had accomplished in my life, I read Psalm 40:10 to inspire me. I wanted to say to the Lord, "I will go where You want me to go and say what You want me to say." Maybe my words would alienate me from family and friends. Maybe my words would cause people to think bad things about me. Maybe people would judge or mock me. Maybe I'd live in shame and embarrassment if I dared to speak about Jesus.

What holds you back from speaking, writing, or any form of expressing God's work in your life? What's your Shadow Narrative of silence?

Have you said any of these statements or others like them to yourself before?

I'm a terrible writer.

I'm a terrible speaker.

God could never use me in the lives of others.

I don't know enough about the Bible to speak about God.

People will tease me and I will lose friendships if I am honest about my walk with Jesus.

I'm afraid I'm sinning if I want attention for speaking about Jesus publicly.

I don't want spiritual attack, so I'm going to stay quiet and mind my own business.

I don't want people to think I'm a fanatic.

People will judge me and think I'm narrow-minded and judgmental.

God uses ordinary, unschooled people (Acts 4:13). God uses the "worst of sinners" to proclaim His power and glory. Do you believe that God could use you?

Transform the above statements into a Savior Story like this:

God gives me words to write.

God gives me words to say.

God can use me in the lives of others.

God can use my limited knowledge to proclaim Him.

God is more important than my reputation or the potential loss of friendships.

God is able to humble me if my speaking or writing bring fame and money.

God will rescue me from every evil attack.

God tells me to "never be lacking in zeal" (Rom. 12:11).

God will help me grow in compassion, empathy, and love as I explain myself to those who oppose Christianity.

Will you agree with God that your silence and concealment of His work in your life isn't His plan for you? Did it ever occur to you that your Savior Stories will bring hope to someone else? Has it ever occurred to you that God gave you your Savior Story to instruct others, to enlarge their view of Jesus, to inspire them, to warn them, to make them braver, and to challenge them?

Your story might also give people permission to ask questions that scare them, to struggle with their own shadows, and to truly heal a wound inside of them. As Mary Pipher explains, our stories and personal essays are how we "turn our own lives into teachable moments for others."[1]

Think about the personal stories others have told you that have changed you. How has another's Savior Story provided you with hope or healing?

Think about how you intersect with certain people. What if the Savior Story your life tells happens to match exactly what they need to hear right now?

Who needs to hear your Savior Story?

STUCK IN YOUR STORY

The next question to address is for those who feel "stuck in their story." As we come to the last week of this study of Ephesians, let me provide you with one of my favorite coaching questions to help people grow. *Where are you stuck?*

As you look through the verbs of Ephesians—*included, chosen, seated, strengthened, renewed, filled, and proclaiming*—which identity do you inhabit fully, and which one still feels like a foreign country to you (something you've heard about but can't imagine making a home in)?

I once lived in the memories of loss and betrayal and regret. I lived in the pain of single days, and single events, that I couldn't erase from my mind. I was trapped in a perpetual state of grieving, anger, and bitterness over a few specific events in my life.

And I was stuck. I was stuck in my story.

I didn't just need a new way to reframe the pain in my life. I needed an encounter with a Savior.

I was crying on a bed in a strange city where we had traveled once again for a ministry assignment. I was stewing inside about particular memories. I felt like something was permanently broken inside of me and that I had come to a place in my life where I could go no further without some kind of divine intervention. I knew God intended to compose a great story out of my life—a Savior Story of His love and power and provision—but I didn't know how to become part of that plot line. Instead, I lived in the various wounds of my past.

In a very special moment of prayer—one I have only shared with three people and never in a public setting—I imagined I was in the throne room of God Himself. I'm not exactly sure what was happening to me; I just knew that I was praying to Jesus and felt more enveloped by His love and power than I ever had before or since. In this encounter in prayer, I imagined I was approaching God, and He was listening to me. I thought about the angels surrounding the throne room of God and the beauty and power of Jesus Christ and God the Father.

In this moment with God—the most authentic moment I have ever had with Jesus—I came to Him for healing. I asked Him to heal all the things that were holding me back from the story He was writing for me. I brought every memory to Him, one by one—all those places keeping me stuck in my story—and it felt like God took all the dark power out of them.

I realized that Jesus was with me as I carried all those memories to Him and talked to Him about my fear, loneliness, and sadness. As I talked with Jesus, I knew that He loved me more than I could ever understand and that He would continue to write my healing story and bring me safely into eternity when my time on earth ended. I'm not sure how I knew this, but God filled me with the faith to believe in God's goodness, love, kindness, and redemption. I felt renewed and healed.

In that moment of feeling so new and healed, I asked God one question that had been on my heart since I was a little girl. You would think I would have asked about all the mysteries of the universe or something about the future, but instead, I asked Him:

"God, what do You think of my writing?" And in my soul, I felt God's delight. After this special day in July 2011, God launched me into a public ministry of writing and speaking. He healed my Shadow Narrative, and I began to live a different Savior Story of proclaiming God's power, goodness, and love everywhere I went.

Where do you feel stuck in your story? Do you need an encounter with Jesus regarding some part of your past? Go to God in a moment of your most authentic and raw prayer. Tell Him where you feel stuck and what needs to heal if you are to move forward in your life.

We also become stuck in our story when we don't realize there's a different story to live. God used Ephesians—more than any other book of the Bible—to cause my relationship with Him to flourish. I was reading a different story for my life in this book. This small letter sparks a revolution in the soul and invites us to live from a totally different story of what it means to be human and yet invaded by the divine presence of Jesus by the Holy Spirit. When we read Ephesians and internalize its truths, we live differently. We live as *included, chosen, seated, filled, renewed, strengthened, and proclaiming.*

These characteristics of our new life in Christ, however, arrive as a beautiful gift each new morning that we might choose to receive or not. Unfortunately, many of us push the gift away and live instead in old realities, old identities, and old stories. It's easier that way. It's familiar and understandable. It's comfortable and known. In many ways, our lives become what psychologists call "habituated." Habituation means we simply become used to our surroundings, no matter how unhealthy or joyless. We normalize unhealthy ways of being because we simply cannot conceive of health and well-being. Our old story is familiar and comfortable. Our old story isn't so terrible, right? *We become used to our lives.*

We become habituated to loneliness.

We become habituated to rejection.

We become habituated to jealousy and comparison.

We become habituated to weariness and emptiness.

We become habituated to sin and stay in our old selves.

We become habituated to self-effort and self-direction.

We become habituated to our speech patterns of silence or complaining.

Ask God to show you any areas of your life where you are habituated to a Shadow Narrative. Perhaps you are stuck in your story because you need to see what life could look like if you were set free.

ENLARGING YOUR SAVIOR STORIES

As you look back over the last weeks, you wrote a collection of Savior Stories that you might now combine with an introduction of your Shadow Narrative. You can condense these stories into three-minute spoken testimonies or five hundred written words (like a blog post) to quickly pass on to others. Begin with the "before picture" and the Shadow Narrative, and then move quickly into the Savior Story of how God taught you to live in the reality of the included, chosen, seated, strengthened, renewed, filled, and proclaiming story. You can also use art or other forms of proclaiming like songs or poems.

This kind of work we've accomplished through Ephesians now might become a model of how you'll now gather more and more Savior Stories as you read Scripture and continue to grow in your faith. You have so many tools now available to you as you read God's Word to learn, including your before and after contrasts, your lists of questions (who, what, where, why, how, when), and the dominant images you wish to use to recall God's work in your life. You can always ask, "How might I live differently in light of this description? How can I experience Jesus here? What do I need to confess that's hindering this reality in my life?"

The Bible offers a comprehensive way to organize our lives and how we think about our world. Reading it daily with the goal of connecting with Jesus, learning from the Holy Spirit, and internalizing its truths, conforms us to Christ and leads us to freedom, peace, and increasing joy.

Some people say that a Spirit-filled life is a Word-filled life, meaning the Holy Spirit primarily uses the Bible to speak to us personally and shape our lives. Yet many people have no regular or systematic way of reading the Bible or applying its truths to their lives. They don't know how to write their Savior Stories because they honestly don't know anything about Jesus or what He is doing in their souls or in the world. They don't regularly learn from Scripture on their own.

When people ask me how I have time to read God's Word, I might say, "Well, how do you have time to eat?" In other words, we plan our days around that which we feel is most vital. We prioritize what we believe we need most of all. Just as we need daily food, we need a daily intake of God's Word.

I plan for my morning coffee. I make sure it's measured out. I make sure I have my favorite mug cleaned and ready. I have special creamer. Nobody messes with my morning coffee routine. I know without coffee, I fall apart. I'm not myself. I don't have the energy I need, and I view the world through that tired, moody, angry lens.

I know women who plan for their daily quiet time with Jesus. They make sure the house is quiet, so they set their alarms for 5:00 a.m. They make sure they have the books, pens, and journals they need. They sit in a special chair. They ask that nobody interrupt their special time with Jesus. Without it, they know they fall apart. They aren't themselves. They don't have the energy they need, and they view the world through a tired, moody, angry lens.

What do we have to believe is true about God's Word to develop a daily habit of reading it?

As I read God's Word, I find that the Holy Spirit faithfully leads me to confess sin, to surrender more deeply, and to worship Jesus more and more in the splendor of His Holiness. Our Savior Stories aren't finished; God is still working and still bearing fresh fruit through our lives.

Make a list of hints of new Savior Stories Jesus is beginning to write in your life in new areas. How is He redeeming your past or your weaknesses? How is He continuing to turn your darkness into light?

CONFRONTING THE SHADOWS AROUND US

In our last two days together, let's move beyond our personal Savior Stories and think more broadly about our community, nation, and world. Answer these questions as a way to consider how God might lead you into increasing ministry to bless and heal, helping others discover and proclaim their Savior Stories. Think about different ethnicities, age groups, abilities, education levels, or anything else that the Holy Spirit brings to your mind as a group whose lives burden you.

• Which people or group most need to feel included right now?

• Which people or group live as rejected and not chosen?

• Who needs to know they are seated at the Greatest Table with the Greatest King?

• Who needs strengthening? Who needs the fullness of God and immeasurably more of Him?

- Which people or group would you like to challenge to experience the renewal of God?

- Which people or group could you see having impact if they understood how to live a Spirit-filled life?

- Which people or group, if trained to proclaim, would you want to see telling their Savior Stories?

Jesus came to seek and save the lost (Luke 19:10). God is near to the broken-hearted and saves those who are crushed in spirit (Ps. 34:18). Isaiah 58:10 offers this exhortation: "If you spend yourselves in behalf of the hungry and satisfy the needs of the oppressed, then your light will rise in the darkness, and your night will become like the noonday."

When I look at my community and world, I find my heart drawn toward certain people and certain groups. I ask God for wisdom, creativity, insight, and energy to move out into more and more ministry to the people and groups He places on my heart. Maybe you feel drawn to preschoolers or the elderly, graduate students or teens. Maybe you feel drawn toward the homeless, inmates, or those in the hospital.

Our stories aren't for us alone. We share our Savior Stories, we listen to others tell theirs, and we now help others tell their own stories of God rescuing and healing. Wherever we go—and whatever we're doing—we proclaim and invite others to proclaim their Savior Stories.

As we go, we worship Jesus Christ—this magnificent God who includes, chooses, seats, strengthens, renews, fills, and proclaims through us.

THE STORY YOU'RE MOST KNOWN FOR

Choose just one of your Savior Stories and spend some time today crafting it into a short (500 words or 3–5 minutes) presentation to showcase to your Bible study group.

Of all the verbs we've studied, which one mattered most?

Which verb represents the deepest transformation in your heart?

Which story makes Jesus a marvelous hero?

Who was I before?

How did I meet Jesus here?

What happened next?

Who am I now?

Which Bible verse best encapsulates my Savior Story?

And now, trust Jesus to use you to bless others with the story He has written, and is writing, of your life through Ephesians. I'm so excited for you! I'm so excited for those who will hear or read your stories. Thank you for taking this journey with me. Now, we are part of one another's stories forever.

APPENDIX A

WRITING TIPS FROM A WRITING PROFESSOR

"There is no greater agony than bearing an untold story inside you."
—Maya Angelou, *I Know Why the Caged Bird Sings*

I assign my students a handbook called *How to Write with Flair* that offers easy ways to immediately improve our writing. This book has become the bread and butter of my courses and the content of writing seminars both for the corporate and ministry world.[1] In just forty-five minutes, I help people who feel like terrible, incompetent writers transform their writing into something authentic, vivid, and irresistible to read. I tell students that every paragraph needs five things: *strong verbs, advanced grammar to create a written voice, varied sentence lengths and openings, cleverness, and an awareness of audience.* For the purposes of this Bible study, let's take in just a few quick areas.

1. Compose your sentences for readers to let them see, taste, feel, hear, or smell whenever possible. Writers call this "sensory detail."

2. Think of yourself as a character in a story. What does she wear? What does she eat? What kinds of things does this character say? What's unique about this character that would allow the reader to see her?

3. When you write any sentence, compose it around a verb (the action word) that gives the reader a mood (how to feel) and an image (what to see). For example, if you wanted to describe your setting of a brisk autumn day, you might say:

   The leaves are on the ground.

Like most people, this writer chose a weak verb (are) that provides no emotion and offers no image to transport us. Other weak verbs to avoid include *is, was, were, has, have, had, seems, appears, exists* (see how you don't feel anything or see anything when you read that list?).

But now try blessing and delighting the reader with a stunning verb. Meander through the alphabet and find twenty-six vivid verbs: The leaves (arrive, blanket, cavort, dance, explode, fan, grapple, hover, illustrate, jet-ski, kiss, lavish, mourn, nod, oscillate, pummel, query, ricochet, skip, tousle, usher, vacillate, wander, xanthate, yearn, or zip) on the ground. As you write your Shadow Narratives and Savior Stories, practice using vivid verbs, and you'll find your writing takes on new energy.

4. Next, practice toggling advanced grammar to create a written voice. A written voice refers to the way we feel we connect with you as a real person in your words; we sense an authentic, actual person in the writing. Voice means the *sum of stylistic choices you make about each paragraph including verbs and grammar.* Try using a semicolon to connect two sentences; the second sentence should explain or amplify the first (like this!). Try these techniques: use a colon for a list or definition, a parenthesis to offer side commentary (like a whisper to the reader), and dashes for a shout. A dash—something underused but so power-ful—highlights whatever sits within those dashes. When we write sentences using various kinds of punctuation, we create rhythm, like music.

5. Change your sentence lengths and openings. Great writers know a secret: varying sentence lengths and openings creates a voice. That's it! So easy! Do you feel like you're hearing my voice? Like I'm actually here? That's my *written voice*. And guess what—the voice comes through because of the lengths of my sentences and how I choose to begin them. In other words, I start with varied openings. Also, if I have a very long sentence that holds much information for the reader, the very next sentence can offer a break. So I'll use a short sentence. I'll pare down to bare bones. I'll get sparse. Try writing a long sentence, a medium-length sentence, another very long sentence, and then a three- to five-word sentence. Suddenly, you'll hear a voice. Can you hear mine?

Other tips for writing down your stories:

Set up a writing environment you enjoy. Maybe you love lighting candles, pouring a mug of steaming, rich coffee, arranging pillows on an office chair. Stack up any resources you think you'll need (Bible, dictionary, commentary, thesaurus). You might type sometimes and other times write by hand.

Choose a time of day when you feel your best. I write between 9:00–11:00 a.m., but I have friends who feel most awake and energized at 9:00 p.m.

It doesn't have to be amazing. Not many of us are called to write the next best-seller. Perfectionism kills creativity. Your writing doesn't have to be perfect. It won't be perfect. It won't be your best work, and that's okay.

Finally, like those who exercise regularly, remind yourself how writing benefits your brain and your mental health. The activity of putting down words to your experience increases joy and well-being according to the best research available.

Get started! Even if you just write three sentences today, get started and see what God will do as you faithfully begin to record His activity in your life. I can't wait to see what happens as you do!

APPENDIX B

IDEAS FOR SHARING YOUR SAVIOR STORIES

Now that you have a collection of stories, think about ways to use them.

• Invite neighbors—both Christians and not-yet believers—to a gathering such as a coffee date, luncheon, dinner, or dessert with the express purpose of sharing your Savior Stories. Think about creating your own "firelight talk" phenomenon in your neighborhood where folks gather to share life stories of hardship and tales of wisdom, warning, and healing. When it's your turn, your stories will focus on Jesus, and people will want to hear more and more.

• Begin a blog or online journal that you post through social media. Blogging your Savior Stories means that people all over the world can click on your link and read a story that helps them inhabit Scripture and God's work in your life. When I posted my first blog on *Live with Flair*, five people read it. Now, thousands read daily.

• Try your hand at podcasting. Think about performing your Savior Story as a three- to five-minute monologue. Practice making your sentences sound exciting, and remember to speak at a normal tone (not shouting or whispering).

• Offer to present a Savior Story at retreats, conferences, Sunday school classes, or events at your local church. Get comfortable speaking on a stage and with a microphone (either in your hand or attached to your head or clothing). Take notes with you, but remember that the best Savior Stories come across as natural and from the heart. I recommend memorizing your story. And don't forget all age groups! Maybe the youth group needs your story or the senior citizens who meet for breakfast each week. Maybe you could use puppets for the preschoolers or perform your story for the young professionals in your church.

• Compile the Savior Stories of your Bible study into a keepsake booklet and then share them with family members and friends far and wide.

• Submit your Savior Story to editors of Christian magazines or websites. If you visit the website of Christian magazines, you can normally find a tab about "submissions" or contacting the editors. On this page, the editors often ask for kinds of stories they are looking for (including word count and payment). You can follow the directions there for how to submit your story idea.

• At your own family dinner table, share a Savior Story around the table.

• Use Facebook live stream or a YouTube video to talk to a viewing audience about God's work in your life. Remember to use hand gestures, facial expressions, and good eye contact.

• Plan a holiday party (Christmas, Easter, other) to invite neighbors and have a spotlight moment for Savior Stories related to the holiday. During the holidays, people experience the most loneliness and isolation. Your Savior Story of included, chosen, and seated might bring these people to the Savior, who wants them to belong to the family of God.

• Go find brokenhearted, hurting, or forgotten people in your community to encourage with Savior Stories and to train them how to tell their own Savior Stories. Think about community centers for homeless or impoverished youth, senior living centers, or any groups that stir your heart.

IF YOU FEEL NERVOUS

I read in 1 Corinthians 1:5 that in Jesus I "have been enriched in every way—with all kinds of speech and with all knowledge" and that we "do not lack any spiritual gift as [we] eagerly wait for our Lord Jesus Christ to be revealed" (v. 7). Even today before a radio interview or a speaking event, I recite Isaiah 50:4 that God "has given me a well-instructed tongue, to know the word that sustains the weary," and I pray that my words are wise, gracious, and bring favor.

Remember that both Moses and Jeremiah complained about not knowing what to say. I often find myself afraid and uncertain, and I reread Jeremiah 1. Here God appoints Jeremiah to proclaim about Him, and Jeremiah says, "Alas, Sovereign LORD, I do not know how to speak; I am too young" (v. 6). God responds and says, "You must go to everyone I send you to and say whatever I command you. Do not be afraid of them, for I am with you and will rescue you," and later, "Get yourself ready! Stand up and say to them whatever I command you. . . . They will fight against you but will not overcome you, for I am with you and will rescue you" (vv. 7–8, 17, 19). And remember, Moses kept begging for God to send someone else, and God said twice, "I will help you speak and will teach you what you should say" (Ex. 4:12; 4:15).

I'm so excited about your Savior Stories!

NOTES

Before You Begin

1. Klyne Snodgrass, *The NIV Application Commentary: Ephesians* (Grand Rapids: Zondervan, 1996), 17.

2. Ibid.

3. Robert J. Marzano, Debra J. Pinkering, and Jane E. Pollock, *Classroom Instruction that Works: Research-Based Strategies for Increasing Student Achievement* (Alexandria, VA: Association for Supervision & Curriculum Development, 2001), 73.

4. James W. Pennebaker, PhD, and John F. Evans, EdD, *Expressive Writing: Words that Heal: Using Expressive Writing to Overcome Traumas and Emotional Upheavals, Resolve Issues, Improve Health, and Build Resilienc*e (Enumclaw, WA: Idyll Arbor, 2014), 18–26.

5. Ibid., 26.

6. Daniel J. Siegel, *Mindsight: The New Science of Personal Transformation* (New York: Bantam Books, 2010), 187.

Week One: Included

1. Walter A. Elwell and Robert W. Yarbrough, *Encountering the New Testament: A Historical and Theological Survey* (Grand Rapids: Baker Publishing Group, 2013), 292.

2. Andrew F. Walls, "The Ephesian Moment: At a Crossroads in Christian History," in *The Cross-Cultural Process in Christian History* (New York: Orbis Books, 2002), 79.

3. F. Lionel Young, *A New Kind of Missionary: What Every Christian Needs to Know about the Global Church* (Toronto: Clements Publishing Group, 2012), 11.

4. Walls, 81.

5. George E. Vaillant, *Triumphs of Experience: The Men of the Harvard Grant Study* (Cambridge, MA: Harvard UP, 2012), 9.

6. Ibid., 37.

7. Katie Hafner, "Researchers Confront an Epidemic of Loneliness," *New York Times*, September 5, 2016, http://www.nytimes.com/2016/09/06/health/lonliness-aging-health-effects.html.

8. Justin Worland, "Why Loneliness May Be the Next Big Public-Health Issue," *TIME*, March 18, 2015, http://time.com/3747784/loneliness-mortality/.

9. Teghan Beaudette, "Nearly 70% of University Students Battle Loneliness During School Year, Study Says," *CBC News*, September 9, 2016. http://www.cbc.ca/news/canada/manitoba/university-loneliness-back-to-school-1.3753653.

10. Amy Banks with Leigh Ann Hirschman, *Wired to Connect: The Surprising Link Between Brain Science and Strong, Healthy Relationships* (New York: Penguin, 2016), 3.

11. Ibid., 3.

12. Stephanie Cacioppo et al, "Loneliness: Clinical Import and Interventions," *Perspectives on Psychological Science* 10 (2015): 238.

13. Laurie A. Theek and Jennifer A. Mallow, "The Development of LISTEN: A Novel Intervention for Loneliness," *Open Journal for Nursing* 2 (2015): 137.

14. Capioppo, 242.

15. David Aaker and Jennifer L. Aaker, "What Are Your Signature Stories?" *California Management Review* 58 (2016): 2.

16. Mary Pipher, *Writing to Change the World* (New York: Penguin, 2006), 45.

17. "The Best Global Brands of 2015," *Interbrand Rankings*, http://interbrand.com/best-brands/best-global-brands/2015/ranking/, and also Nik Rawlinson, "The History of Apple," April 1, 2016, http://www.macworld.co.uk/feature/apple/history-of-apple-steve-jobs-what-happened-mac-computer-3606104/.

18. Peter Scazzero, *The Emotionally Healthy Leader: How Transforming Your Inner Life Will Deeply Transform Your Church, Team, and the World* (Grand Rapids: Zondervan, 2015), 55.

19. Carl Jung, *The Archetypes and the Collective Unconscious* (Princeton, NJ: Princeton UP, 1969), 284.

Week Two: Chosen

1. *Billboard* (New York: Nielsen Business Media, September 28, 1985), 40.

2. Wikipedia contributors, "Aileen Quinn," *Wikipedia, The Free Encyclopedia,* https://en.wikipedia.org/w/index.php?title=Aileen_Quinn&oldid=752969872.

3. Kenneth S. Wuest, *Wuest's Word Study from the Greek New Testament for the English Reader, Volume One: Mark, Romans, Galatians, Ephesians, and Colossians* (Grand Rapids: Eerdmans, 1953), 29–31.

4. Marcus Peter Johnson, *One with Christ: An Evangelical Theology of Salvation* (Wheaton, IL: Crossway, 2013), 31.

5. Jonathan Edwards, *Christians: A Chosen Generation, a Royal Priesthood, an Holy Nation, and a Peculiar People: Revised Edition (With Active Table of Contents)*, 1834, Kindle edition.

6. Eugene Peterson, *Practice Resurrection: A Conversation on Growing Up in Christ* (Grand Rapids: Eerdmans, 2010), 58.

7. Amanda Chan, "This Is Why Rejection Hurts (And How to Cope)," *The Huffington Post*, March 16, 2014, http://www.huffingtonpost.com/2014/03/13/rejection-coping-methods-research_n_4919538.html.

8. Diane Swanbrow, "Study Illuminates the Pain of Social Rejection," *Michigan News*, March 25, 2011, http://ns.umich.edu/new/releases/8332-study-illuminates-the-pain-of-social-rejection.

Week Three: Seated

1. Heather Holleman, *Seated with Christ: Living Freely in a Culture of Comparison* (Chicago: Moody Publishers, 2014). Portions of this chapter excerpted from this book by permission from the publisher.

2. Doug Stevenson, "Signature Stories," guest blog post on *BradMontgomery.com*, July 1, 2006, http://www.bradmontgomery.com/guest-speakers/doug-stevenson/signature-stories/.

3. Isidore Singer and Cyrus Adler, "Temple: Administration and Service," *Jewish Encyclopedia: A Descriptive Record of the History, Religion, Literature, and Customs of the Jewish People from the Earliest Times to the Present Day*, (New York: Funk & Wagnalls) 1901, http://www.jewishencyclopedia.com/articles/14303-temple-administration-and-service-of. Here, we read that "half of the chamber extended outside the court to the 'ḥel,' a kind of platform surrounding the courts, which was considered as secular, in contrast to the sacred premises within, where the priests were not allowed to sit down."

4. Charles Spurgeon, "The Only Atoning Priest," *A Sermon Delivered on Lord's Day Morning, February 4th, 1872, at the Metropolitan Tabernacle, Newington*, Sermon 1034:73, http://www.spurgeon.org/index/c18.htm.

5. The first mention of the Round Table appears in writing from the French Poet Robert Wace in *Roman de Brut* (c.1155) based on Geoffrey of Monmouth's *History of the Kings of Britain* (c. 1136) that describes the history and mythology of Great Britain.

6. *Hayden Planetarium Guide*, as quoted by Lorrie Moore in the front matter of her book *A Gate at the Stairs* (New York: Vintage, 2010). To confirm the source of this quote, I contacted the Hayden Planetarium staff. While they could not direct me to the original source, they said, "[the quote] is factually correct. The planetarium is a spherical space, with the floor mildly sloping upward. The images projected into the domed ceiling and upper part of the wall can be seen equally by everyone." Email to the author, October 25, 2014.

Week Four: Strengthened

1. Billy Graham, "The Ultimate Protection," in *Unto the Hills: A Daily Devotional* (Nashville: Thomas Nelson, 2010), 3.

2. Walter Henrichsen and Howard Hendricks, *Disciples Are Made Not Born: Helping Others Grow into Maturity in Christ* (Colorado Springs: David C. Cook, 1988), 47.

3. Anupum Pant, "The Role of Wind in a Tree's Life," *AweSci: Science Everyday*, December 28, 2014, http://awesci.com/the-role-of-wind-in-a-trees-life/.